The HIKER'S GUIDE
To The
CENTRAL SIERRAS

Shaver, Florence, & Huntington

Lakes Region

Thirty-Five Day Hikes

Get your asses out here + hike!

*Written
by*
Greg Goodman
and
Pam Geisel
Illustrated by
Andrea Goodman

Arg + Andy

Merry Christmas!

Copyright © 2002,
ISBN 0-9721434-0-8

Book Layout & Design
by
Ernie (Hergie) Hergenroeder

DEDICATION

The Central Sierra Hiking Guide is dedicated to Colonel Ashton Hallett and Major Peter Ordway. Co-founders of the Ordway's Raiders, Ash and Peter intrepidly led the Raiders into the wilderness world of beauty and joy they knew intimately. For Ash and Peter's love of challenge, excitement, and the outdoors, this book is a metaphor of their memory carried forth.

"Here's to it, and to it again! If we don't get to it to do it, we won't get to it to do it again!"

Ashton Hallett

Peter Ordway

*Illustration of the proposed Central Sierra
Historical Society museum.*

HENRY DAVID THOREAU

"I think that I cannot preserve my health and spirits, unless I spend four hours a day at least,- and it's commonly more than that,- sauntering through the woods and over the hills and fields, absolutely free from all worldly engagements. You may safely say, A penny for your thoughts, or a thousand pounds. When some-times I am reminded that the mechanics and shopkeepers stay in their shops not only all the forenoon, but all the afternoon too, sitting with crossed legs, so many of them,- as if the legs were made to sit upon, and not to stand or walk upon,- I think that they deserve some credit for not having committed suicide long ago."

Reprinted from "Walking"

ACKNOWLEDGMENTS

Many in the Shaver Lake community have worked to help make this book possible. The Shaver Lake Volunteers have given many days of loving labor to the task of maintaining the system of trails that we all enjoy. A special thank you to Doug Waugh and Chloe French, Rich and Joy Bagley, Mike Asire, Ben and Betsy Casillas, Monroe and Elaine Clark, John Harshman, Lee and Jean Larsen, Charlotte Meier, Bob Penman, and Rod and Marsha Weins. We, too, recognize and thank the many hikers that patiently walked beside us as we tramped along recording field notes. Sometimes they pushed the mileage wheel, but, most of all, they were great company. Thank you: Bob Yeatts; Tim and Pam Geisel and dogs, Sage and Sharrona; Jack and Deby Grisonti and dogs, Skylar and Fury; Laura Bava; Evert and Priscilla Craft; Billy and Raylene Davis; Joan and Ray Scannell; Melinda Friedman and Michael Hallett; Becky Yeatts and her dog, Shaver; Bob and Greg Paul; Carrie Stjerne; Chris Atkinson; Terri Swartz and Nancy Wise; Tyler Stjerne and Elaine Berry; Shirley Mizener; Fred and Patty Kruger; Carol Street; Tom, Debbie, and Linda Lindstrom; Jean and Lee Larson, Russ Westman; and Mark Barville.

We would also like to recognize Plua Her. Plua's work on the trails surrounding Camp Edison add greatly to the walker's enjoyment and safety. Plua was the first trail's coordinator for the Southern California Edison Company. Her enthusiasm and love of nature enhanced the entire project.

We thank John Mount for his visionary leadership. As the land's manager for Southern California Edison Company, he has directed many of the programs that make the Shaver Lake property as beautiful and accessible as it is today. An interview with John is included in this edition. In addition, his assistant, Rich Bagley, has contributed greatly to the trail's volunteers program. He directed the daily operation of the land management program, and his leadership in the development of the trail's system is incalculable. Thanks, also, to Hergie for his artistic and production assistance.

TABLE OF CONTENTS

INTRODUCTION TO HIKING

"In the woods, we return to reason and faith.
There I feel that nothing can befall me in life which
nature cannot repair."

Ralph Waldo Emerson

Welcome to the Huntington, Florence, and Shaver Lake region and the natural beauty that surrounds the Central Sierra. For over the past hundred years, individuals have sought adventure, employment, and recreation within the wilderness and forests that characterize this land. As you ramble about, you, too, become a part of the experience of Huntington, Florence, and Shaver and its surrounding beauty. A new world of beauty will open itself up to you. And in this world, there is much to explore and learn about the history, flora, and fauna. Those seeking more information about the history of Shaver Lake should join the Central Sierra Historical Society, visit the museum, and read Gene Rose's book, *Reflections of Shaver Lake.*

This book is for the visiting hiker and those curious to explore either on cross-country ski, snowshoe, or, in some cases wheelchair. The trips described within this book are varied in both length and difficulty. The book is particularly valuable for the frequent visitor or resident because the trips herein can fill many days of adventuring in the surrounding hills.
The trail descriptions include how to get there, mileage of each trip, and estimates of the amount of time required for each walk. These distances and estimates are approximate. Although we walked many of the trails with a measuring wheel, some of the trails we just walked. The time that it takes you to cover the same ground that we walked may vary. Some days we were fleet footed, other days we were just pokey.
The point of the book is to get you out on the trail and to enjoy the beauty surrounding Huntington, Florence, and Shaver Lakes.
Many of the trails described in this book are on the property of the

1

Southern California Edison Company. Southern California Edison Company owns 15,000 acres in the town of Shaver Lake. Because the company policy of public access and their work to develop top quality recreational facilities are so essential to the visitor and residents' access and enjoyment of the local environment, Southern California Edison Company deserves special recognition. According to Southern California Edison Company research, 600,000 person/days of land use are counted each year.

Your contribution of respect for nature adds to the beauty we all enjoy. The best way to show your appreciation of the open land use policy employed by Southern California Edison Company and your National Forest is to follow the "Carry-in/Carry-out " rule. Anything that you bring with you needs to leave with you. Everything! This rule protects the natural beauty for all. Those wishing to enhance the natural beauty of the area may bring a garbage bag on their walk for removal of items left by those less considerate or conscious of litters unattractiveness.

In addition to aesthetic considerations, the Southern California Edison Company asks that the following rules please be observed while visiting their property.

1. Comply with all state and local laws.
2. Gas stoves and barbecues are permitted in campgrounds and picnic areas with permanent cooking grills installed. Please put all fires out when not in attendance.
3. Smoking is permitted in vehicles and areas cleared of all flammable materials for at least 10 feet.
4. Most areas are open for day use until 10:00 p.m. Camp Edison and Dorabella Campgrounds are available for camping and overnight sleeping. Night fishing is permitted on Shaver Lake.
5. Please take all trash back with you.
6. Motor vehicles may be used on maintained roads and selected areas of the lakeshore below high water. Please keep off dirt roads when wet to protect soft roadbeds.
7. Areas behind locked gates are open to non-motorized day use.
8. Please do not block roads, gates, or facilities when parking.

9. Wood-cutting permits are available for personal use. Details are available at Camp Edison.
10. Overnight boat mooring outside of licensed docks, or leaving items on shore overnight is permitted for up to 14 nights per year.
11. Firearm use is permitted in areas with adequate backstops away from lakes, roads, campgrounds, or other recreational use areas. Please do not use trees for targets or backstops. The West Side of Shaver Lake to the top of Mount Stevenson is closed to all shooting including archery and air guns by county ordinance.

Any questions regarding this policy may be answered by a Southern California Edison Company representative at (559) 841-3194.

Almost all of the other walks that are described in this book are on National Forest land. These trips require the same vigilance regarding respect for the environment. The efforts of as many people as possible to mitigate the effect of the less considerate makes the woods a safer and more beautiful place for all!

One of the other keys to the enjoyment of a day in the mountains is the combination of the factors of knowledge, equipment, and experience. This book hopes to provide a bit of the knowledge you will need to have a successful day in the outdoors. However, you are on your own to bring the right (essential) equipment and to make the best decisions as to when to go and when to turn back. Hopefully, you always will be prudent and not push the envelope of caution too far from your vision. Providing a safe trip for yourself, friends, and family adds greatly to the desire to repeat the experience.

There is an abundance of material concerning equipment and technique. My favorite source is The Mountaineers' canon of outdoorsmanship, **Mountaineering: The Freedom of the Hills.** This book covers all of the requisite areas of safety, equipment, route finding, and technique to keep one healthy and enjoying the mountains for years to come.

In lieu of your being 50 miles away from Barnes and Noble or any other reputable bookseller, I will summarize the salient points in the paragraphs that follow. Please heed this disclaimer! There is nothing more important than your decision making. May you always make the wisest ones!

Equipment

In the early years of Sierra exploration there was John Muir with his long coat and rifle. His courageous image lives on, but the styles of today are dramatically different. At a minimum, ten essentials are the foundation for a successful hike. They include:

1. A comfortable day pack
2. A U.S.G.S. topographic survey map
3. A compass
4. A flashlight in good working order
5. A first aid kit including a whistle
6. Extra food
7. Extra clothing, including rain gear
8. Water
9. Matches
10. A pocket knife

By having these items with you on your walk, you will, as the old boy scouts admonished, be prepared. I take great comfort in having enough "stuff" with me to be able to face an unexpected night out or just an after-lunch chill.

Beyond the "ten essentials," I prefer to bring an extra, dry shirt for the summit. Although cotton makes a comfortable choice for a hot, dry day, I prefer polypropylene or one of the other wicking synthetic fibers. Warm and dry are the objectives for a pleasant time in the mountains.

The list of equipment options can go on and on. Equipment freaks can computerize their trek with Global Positioning Systems, buy watches that contain altimeters, or get Gore-Tex undies. Whatever your style or budget, at least bring the basics.

Route Finding

Great efforts have been made to provide you with accurate information and detailed maps. However, you need to orient yourself to the area and your objectives. Some trails are well marked. They have grooves worn in them that a visually impaired individual could negotiate. Other trails are adorned with cairns (rock piles) or ducks (rock stacks). Occasionally, a trail will have a blaze (an ax mark or a tree) or a hiker decal. Still, you must be able to locate these marks and identify them. You are your own guide. Nothing helps more than familiarity and the knowledge gained from direct experience. Don't stray beyond your comfort zone!

Things to See

Walking is a pleasure in itself. However, knowing what is around you adds to the overall sense of enjoyment. Recognition of certain plants, trees, and flowers gives you a sense of connection to place. Knowing some of the geology allows you to glimpse the power and age of the Sierra Nevada range. The plants and geology described in this book provide a brief guide to help you recognize some of the more common flora and geologic features you might see on the walks around Shaver and Huntington Lakes.

Wildflowers, Trees, and Shrubs

The plants you see will depend upon the time of year and the elevation that your hike takes you across. For example, the flowers in bloom in early spring such as shooting stars and blue dicks will be rare in late summer. The five-needled white pine will be common on dryer high elevation slopes above 9000 feet, but you will not see it below about 8000 feet

Most of the walks will generally take you through two types of mixed conifer forests. At lower elevations from 4000 to 7000 feet, you will walk through the yellow pine forests. Yellow pines are the group of three needled pine species. The most significant trees include the ponderosa pine, sugar pine, incense cedar, white fir, black oak and canyon live oak. The shrubs you will see include Mariposa manzanita, green-leaf manzanita, Sierra gooseberry, bear clover and bush chinquapin. At 6,000 feet and above, the lodge-pole-red fir forest is dominant. The main species include red fir, Jeffrey pine and lodgepole pine, mountain whitethorn, and Sierra juniper. The plant communities blend at middle elevations as transitional forest, and you may see a crossover of species.

The wildflowers are varied, and there are hundreds of species to enjoy depending upon the time of year, the elevation, and local habitat. A few of the major species are identified within the text of this book and following is a listing of some of the more common species you might observe. For more detailed plant lists, see the back of this book for a good selection of references.

COMMON WILDFLOWERS

Crimson Columbine (Aquilegia formosa)—Buttercup family (Ranunculaceae)
Flowers have nodding red spurs and yellow centers. Leaves are pinnate, with three lobed leaves. Common in moist shaded areas and along streams. 1-4 feet in height. There is a rare yellow flowering species noted on one of the hikes in this book.

Mountain Marsh Larkspur (Delphinium polycladon)—Buttercup family (Ranunculaceae)
Flowers have 5 petals, with spurred bluish blooms arising on a central spike. Common on moist hillsides. Blooms July-August.

Pussy Paws (Calyptridium umbellatum)—Purslane family (Portulacaceae)
Plant grows 2-5 inches high in a flat cluster with reddish spatula like leaves. Blooms are rounded fuzzy pinkish clusters in terminal clusters. Common in open, flat areas.

Miner's Lettuce (Montia perfoliata)—Purslane family (Portulacaceae)
Leaves are fleshy and umbrella shaped. Flowers are pale pink and arise from what appears to be the center of the leaf. Common in moist, shaded areas. Blooms Spring to July.

Western Dog Violet (Viola adunca)—Violet family (Violaceace)
Heart shaped leaves with erect stems. Flowers pale to deep violet with 5 petals. Common in moist wooded areas with blooming March to August.

Shelton's Violet (Viola sheltonii)—Violet family (Violaceace)
Common yellow violet with fan shaped, pinnate leaves, which are further, subdivided. Plant grows 1-2 inches and blooms April to

July. There are several other yellow violet species common in the Sierra Nevada as well.

Snow Plant (Sacodes sanguinea)—Wintergreen family (Pyrolaceae)
This plant is a saprophyte that grows as soon as the snow begins to clear in pine forests. Grows 4-12 inches with bright red waxy candle shape. Blooms May to July.

Shooting Stars (Dodecatheon jeffreyi)—Primrose family (Primulaceae)
Broad leaves with pink flowers with 4 or 5 back curved petals. Grows 1-2 feet in wet mountain meadow areas. Blooms May-August.

Broadleafed Lupine (Lupinus latifolius)—Pea family (Leguminosae)
There are many species of lupine. Most have 5-7 leaflets with blue pea-like flowers. This common lupine grows 1-4 feet in moist wooded areas. Blooms April-August.

Fireweed (Epilobium angustifolium)—Evening Primrose family (Onagraceae)
Fireweed has 4 large bright red-purple petals in long terminal spike. Grows 2-9 feet. Common in disturbed areas. Booms June-September.

Queen Anne's Lace (Daucus carota)—Carrot family (Umbelliferae)
Common plant with creamy white flowers in flat-topped umbels with feathery green fern-like leaves. Grows 1-5 feet. Blooms May-October. To distinguish from other similar plants look for dark flower found in the center of the lacy white umbel of flowers.

Poison Hemlock (Conium maculatum)—Carrot family (Umbelliferae)
The stem of this plant is spotted purple and has a single tall stem of flowers in an umbel. Leaves are fern-like. Grows 2-10 feet in disturbed areas. Considered very poisonous. Blooms March-September.

Mountain Phlox (Phlox diffusa)—Phlox family (Polemoniaceae)
Pink to white flowers often seen in spreading mats. The low shrubby plant has sharp needle like foliage growing 3-12 inches in open places between 3,000 and 14,000 feet. Blooms May-August.

Indian Paintbrush (Castilleja spp.)—Snapdragon family (Scrophulariaceae)
Red tubular flowers clustered among bright colored modified leaves called bracts are typical of this species. Stems typically grow from 1-6 inches or 1-2 feet, depending upon the species. Different species prefer different habitat from dry alpine meadows to moist places. Blooms May-September.

Yellow Monkey Flower (Mimulus guttatus)—Snapdragon family (Scrophulariaceae)
Yellow lipped tubular flowers growing to variable heights of 2 inches to 3 feet. Prefers moist places in low to mid elevations. Blooms March-September.

Showy Penstemon (Penstemon speciosus)—Snapdragon family (Scrophulariaceae)
Blue-purple tubular flowers that grow atop low spreading stems to a height of 2 to 3 feet on open mountain slopes. Blooms May-July.

Western Joe-pye-weed (Eupatorium occidentale)
Pink to purple flowers born in dense clusters on clumped stems. Grows 1-3 feet along mountain stream banks and in forested areas. Blooms July-September.

California Goldenrod (Solidago californica)—Sunflower family (Compositae)
Thick spike like cluster of golden flowers, growing in clumps. Common in open places growing 1-4 feet. Blooms late July-October.

Leafy or Mountain Asters (Aster foliaceus and A. Modestus)—Sunflower family (Compositae)
Common violet-to-blue daisy-like flowers growing 3 feet in wooded areas and mountain meadows. Blooms July-September.

Mules Ears (Wyethia mollis)—Sunflower family (Compositae)
Large oblong leaves with dense white hairs. Large daisy-like flowers are yellow. Grows 1-2 feet on open slopes below 7,000 feet blooms May-August.

Common Yarrow (Achillea millefolium)—Sunflower family (Compositae)
White flowers in flat-topped clusters. Leaves are finely dissected with numerous white hairs on the stem. Grows 1-3 feet. Blooms March-November.

Elegant Brodiaea (Brodiaea elegans)—Amaryllis family (Amaryllidacea)
Blue to violet tubular flowers in clusters atop a long slender stalk. Grows 1-3 feet in open pine forests and on hillsides from March-July.

Mountain Pretty Face (Brodiaea lutea)—Amaryllis family (Amaryllidacea)
Yellow star like flowers in clusters atop long slender stalk. Each sepal has a dark line down the back. Common in pine forests and wooded areas. Grows 6-20 inches. Blooms May-August.

Leopard Lily (Lilium pardalinum)—Lily family (Liliaceae)
Bright orange-red flowers with maroon spots atop a slender stalk. Leaves are lance shaped and are whorled along the stem. Grows 2-4 feet in wet mountain meadows and open woods or along streambanks from May-July.

Mariposa or Sego Lily (Calochortus nuttalli)—Lily family (Liliaceae)
Bowl shaped white or yellowish flowers with brown to purple spot in the center. Leaves long and slender at the base of the stem. Grows 6-15 inches in open areas, slopes and in pine forests. Bloom from May-August.

Corn Lily (Veratrum californicum)—Lily family (Liliaceae)
White flowers in dense clustered spikes atop a thick stem and large leaves that clasp the stem. Large pleat-like veins on the leaves. Plant grows 2-6 feet in wet meadows swamps and stream banks. Blooms from June-August.

Cliff Penstemon (*Penstemon rupicola*)

Andersons Thistle (*Cirsium andersonii*)

Black eyed Susan (*Rudbeckia hirta*)

Blue Elderberry (*Sambucus caerulea*)

10

Dogwood *(Cornus)*

Common Yarrow *(Achillea millefolium)*

Hooker's Onion *(Allium acuminatum)*

Golden Rod *(Solidago california)*

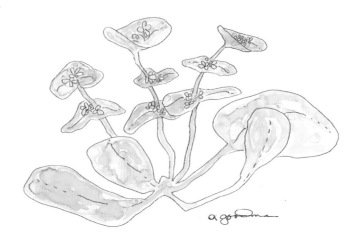

Miner's Lettuce *(Montia perfoliata)*

Mountain Mule Ear *(Wyethia mollis)*

Leafy Aster *(Aster foleacius)*

Pussy Paws *(Calyptridium umbellatum)*

12

Shooting Star *(Dodecatheon Jeffreyi)*

Snow Plant *(Sacodes sanguinea)*

Sierra Lupine *(Lupinus grayi)*

Western Dog Violet *(Viola adunca)*

13

Columbine *(Aquilegia flavescens)*

Indian Paintbrush *(Castilleja)*

Rocky Mountain Iris *(Iris missouriensis)*

Western larkspur *(Delphinium nuttallianum)*

14

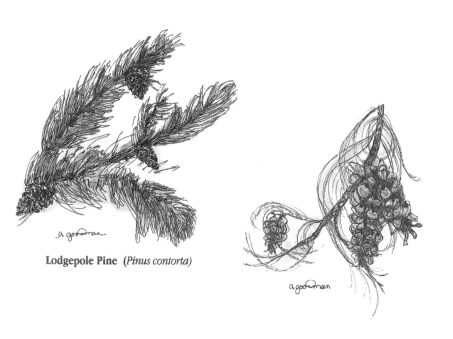

Lodgepole Pine (*Pinus contorta*)

Ponderosa Pine (*Pinus ponderosa*)

COMMON TREES

Evergreen Trees

Ponderosa Pine (Pinus ponderosa)
Ponderosa pine is a common pine growing from British Columbia into Texas and Southern California. It has dark green needles 4-8 inches long that grow in bundles of three (some varieties may only have two or five). The cones are light reddish brown in a cone shape that has a prickly spur at the tip of each cone scale. Often found in mixed forests.

Lodgepole Pine (Pinus contorta var. murrayana)
Lodgepole pines are 2 needle pines that grow at higher elevations from about 7,000 to 11,500 feet. They have short yellowish green needles (1"-2") that are sometimes twisted and small egg shaped cones.

Jeffrey Pine (Pinus jeffreyi)

Jeffrey Pine is a tree distinguished by its fragrant bark that smells like vanilla, or some say pineapple or lemon. It has long bluish needles that grow in bundles of three. It grows usually between 6,000 and 9,000 feet on dry mountain slopes and often in pure stands. The cone is light reddish brown from 5-8 inches long. The nickname "Gentle Jeffrey" comes from the fact that

Jeffrey Pine *(Pinus Jeffreyi)*

when you pick up the cone, it doesn't prickle like the Ponderosa will.

Whitebark Pine (Pinus albicaulis)

Whitebark pine is a smaller pine growing to only 50 feet. Its needles are dull green growing 1-2 inches long in bundles of 5. They are stiff and bunched at the ends of the twigs. The cones are purplish and egg shaped growing to about 1-3 inches long. They are usually found at the higher elevations between 7,000-11,000 feet on dry rocky ridges.

Sugar Pine (Pinus lambertiana)

Sugar pine is the most majestic pine in the area. It is an important lumber tree growing 100-160 feet tall in mixed forests between the elevations of 3,000 to 7,800 feet. They have a tall straight trunk and few branches for much of its length. At maturity, the crown is open and becomes flattened with age. It has long (3-4 inches) blue green needles with white lines in bundles of 5. The cones are very large and long

Sugarpine *(Pinus lambertiana)*

(11-18 inches) and hang from long stalks in the upper branches.

Incense Cedar (Calocedrus decurrens)

The incense cedar is a common tree occurring in the upper transitional mixed forests on mountain slopes and canyons ranging in elevations primarily from 2,500 to 7,500 feet. It can be identified by its flattened scale-like leaves and branchlets. The bark is thick

16

and fibrous with a rich cinnamon-brown color and is broken into longitudinal furrows. Its cones are a delightful bell-shape with two "wings" when open.

California Red Fir (Abies magnifica)
The California Red Fir is a beautiful species with rich reddish-brown bark. It is a large evergreen tree with narrow branches that form into a narrow cone though somewhat rounded at the top. It grows 60-120 feet and can be found at elevations between 6,000 and 9,000 feet in the Shaver/Huntington area. It is distinguished from other conifers by its short (1 inch) upright needles that grow in two rows along twigs on 4 sides. Cones are cylindrical growing 6-8 inches long and purplish brown. Cones grow upright on the higher branches.

Western Juniper (Juniperus occidentalis)
The Sierra or Western juniper is a lovely smallish tree growing 10-60 feet tall. It has open spreading branches when mature and scale like branchlets, which are gray-green in color. The bark is deeply furrowed and shredded looking with a reddish brown color. The cones are berry like and about 1 inch long, blue-black in color with a white film. It is usually found on dryish slopes from 3,000 to 10,000 feet in red fir forests to subalpine forests.

DECIDUOUS TREES

Pacific Dogwood (Cornus nuttallii)
Pacific dogwood is one of the most beautiful trees in this area. It is a small tree growing to 20-30 feet with showy 3-4 inch white blooms in spring. The actual flower is the center greenish button and the creamy white petals are the bracts. The leaves are simple oval, dark green and turn yellow to scarlet in fall. Pacific dogwood is usually found in moist areas in sun or shade in the mixed conifer forests.

Black Oak (Quercus kelloggii)

The black oak is the most common deciduous oak you will find on your walks around the Shaver lake environs. It is a tree with an open crown growing 40-80 feet high. In spring the leaves are greenish red as they unfold. They then become a yellow green. The leaves are 3-6 inches long; have mostly 7 lobes and are toothed at the tips. The acorn is large with the cup covering the bottom half of the fruit. It takes two seasons for the acorn to mature. In the fall the leaves turn bright yellow.

Willow (Salix spp.)

There are many species of willow inhabiting the Shaver-Huntington area. Most grow as a much-branched shrub or tree in thickets along streams or moist areas. Willows are either male or female. The flowers are born in catkins. Willows typically have smooth bark and twig and the leaves are arranged in alternately along the twig.

Manzanita (Arctostaphylos))

COMMON SHRUBS

Manzanita (Arctostaphylos spp.)

The manzanita in this area are very closely related and often hybridize making species distinctions difficult. For lay people, they can be divided into groups based upon whether they have bright or light green leaves or gray-green leaves. Most manzanita are shrubs, but some are prostrate and others can grow into 20-foot trees. The identifying features of manzanita are their persistent simple leathery leaves that are arranged in an alternate fashion along the twigs; their smooth, reddish peeling bark; and their lovely urn shaped white to pinkish flowers. They also have a berry like fruit that looks like a tiny apple. Manzanita is the Spanish word for little apple.

Mountain Whitethorn (Ceanothus cordulatus)
This shrub is very common and as its name suggests is tipped with whitish thorns which may scratch unwary walkers. This shrub is intricately branched with a spreading habit and growing 3-6 feet high. The whole plant has a grayish look to it. It is usually found in dry sloping areas within the mixed conifer forest.

Bush Chinquapin (Castanopsis sempervirens)
This common shrub is low spreading, growing about 2-4 feet high (higher in other areas). The leaves are distinctive. They are evergreen, oblong and yellowish gray-green on the top and some-what wooly and golden or rusty on the underside. The fruit is spiny and contains several small edible nuts.

Blue Elderberry (Sambucus caerulea)
Elderberries are most noticeable in the fall when the berries mature. The berries are dark blue with a white powdery coating in flat-topped clusters. The fruit of this species makes excellent jams, jellies, and wine. There is a red berry species, which doesn't have a white coating and may give you a stomachache if eaten. The leaves of blue elderberry are pinnately compound with 5-7 oval-shaped leaflets, 6-12 inches long. It grows as an upright shrub or small tree, 10-15 feet high. It is usually found in open areas up to 10,000 feet in elevation.

GEOLOGY OF CENTRAL SIERRA NEVADA

The geology of the Sierra Nevada is quite interesting. Detailed books on the formation of the range are listed in the appendix. What you will mostly see are the large granite domes and outcroppings that are typical in much of the Sierra. The Sierra is made up of a large block of granitic rock called a "batholith." The batholith was uplifted and tilted toward the west during the past 10-12 million years with most of the uplifting taking place in the last 3 million years. The uplift occurred primarily along fault lines at the steep eastern base of the range. The tilting effect has created a gentle slope on the West Side, which allows for a slow transition between plant communities. On the eastern side, the slope is very steep and drops off sharply into the Owens Valley.

The most important natural force to influence the shape and appearance of the Sierra today was glaciation. Glaciation occurred during periods beginning about 3 million years ago. The most recent period called the "little ice age" was recorded only 600 years ago. The effect on the Sierra was the formation of wide "U" shaped valleys, the odd placement of large boulders, called "glacial erratics" which seem to have been randomly dropped atop large expanses of granite, the formation of strings of lakes and cirques known as paternosters and development of glacial moraines.

Weathering is another important influence on the development of the Sierra. Though granite is very hard, it does tend to develop fissures that run parallel along the north-south axis and also perpendicular to that axis. The consequence is that granite then tends to break up in large cubes.

The large granite domes that you may see on many of the walks are also a result of weathering and the erosion of overlying sedimentary rock. The removal of this overlying pressure allowed the granite to expand from the inside, causing it to crack in a spherical pattern similar to that of an onion, peeling away, layer by layer. Most notable of these domes are the Kerkoff Dome in Big Creek and the Dinkey Dome on the route to Dinkey Lakes.

Because of the height of the Sierra, a rain shadow effect is created. As the water-laden air currents from the Pacific move up the mountains, it becomes colder and causes precipitation. As it drops over to the East Side of the Sierra, the air is heated and any remaining water is evaporated off. Thus, much more rain falls on the western side and very little falls on the eastern side. This has a major influence on the vegetation and the development of different biotic zones that you will pass through on your walks.

Overnight Use

The walks contained in this guide are intended for day use only. If you are planning on extending your stay, be sure to secure the necessary permits and permissions. National Forest permits are available through:

Pineridge Ranger District
Post Office Box 559
Prather, CA 93651
(559) 855-5360

Be sure to check this number and address before driving to Prather. The Forest Service is continually upgrading its services and facilities to meet public demand.

A group size maximum and other restrictions on the overnight use of the forest apply. Check with the Forest Service to be sure of all the restrictions!

Nuisances: Big and Small

No trip would be complete without its share of adversity to remind you that you are in the woods and not at the Hilton! These pests are found in many forms, large and small. Of the small variety, mosquitoes are among the top pests going. Expect to encounter them and you will be prepared! Being surprised to see the little pests is a prescription for panic. Bring bug repellent, long sleeves, trousers, and a quick wit to combat these rascals.

Another less apparent pest is the funky attitude we are all vulnerable to acquire! It is normal to feel aches and pains on the trail. A sore neck, a strained knee, a stitch in the back all are symptoms of the sadly, unphysical lifestyle we often lead to support ourselves. Unfortunately, most of us are tethered to desks from Monday until Friday, and we don't go to the gym enough, either. That leaves plenty of room for aches and pains.

I contend that these pains are normal. I don't mean to be a Hun about this. I am just saying that, *"ATTITUDE IS CRUCIAL!"* If you expect to feel rotten for some part of the day, it won't come as a surprise or shock you. It is normal. It, too, will pass! You won't enjoy it, but you will survive it. And those around you will survive you better, too.

This is not to say that you should disregard the formation of a blister until it is a festering sore. Altitude sickness is another irritant not to be disregarded. Carrying symptoms such as loss of appetite, nausea, and headaches, the only good cure is to seek lower altitude. Drinking plenty of water will mitigate some of the symptoms, but go down the hill! Try to always use good judgment. Don't just whine about the routine aches that attend your physical playtime! It is still more fun than sitting on the couch. You will have plenty of time for that activity when you hit the nursing home!

Stream water? Some say, "drink it." Others say, "don't." You can decide to filter the water in a commercial pump or bring imported water from France. Whatever your choice, you will get to live with the consequences. Giardia Lamblia, the water born intestinal parasite, can be picked up on a piece of lettuce or from the beautiful brook you are imagining as you read. Rather than belabor this fetid topic, I carry my own water. The point is to drink lots of water. Some physiologists suggest one liter per hour for heavy exercise. They must have bladders the size of the Goodyear blimp! Bears and other potential sources of harm are rare. However, if you encounter a rattlesnake, bear, or other animal, it is best policy to leave them alone. They will probably be just as surprised to see you, as you are to encounter them. Stand your ground if it seems appropriate, or slowly back away. Show as little fear as possible. And no matter what, don't try to run away. That just becomes a chase me game you will lose!

Seeing animals in the outdoors is a big part of the joy. Coyotes, marmots, birds, and other animals put on a show for free. If you see an animal that you consider a threat, stay away.

Finally, if you think you are lost, stay calm. Your wit and attitude are your best allies. Conversely, losing your cool limits your ability to think of a good solution. Stay positive! Adventure is healthy.

THE SHAVER LAKE BASIN

Shaver Lake, as we now view it, is vastly different than the terrain the Mono Indians inhabited in the centuries before the white man came in search of gold and the other rich resources the Central Sierra had held sacred. Beginning with the gold rush of the 1840's and continuing through the logging of the late nineteenth and early twentieth centuries, Shaver has evolved through a variety of land management practices into the landscape that we admire and enjoy today.

A large part of the beauty of Shaver Lake can be attributed to the forest and land management practices of the Southern California Edison (SCE) Company. The Company's land use policies and the supervision of those operations by their manager, John Mount, deserves the community's recognition for their open space and multiple use practices. In the interview that follows, Mr. Mount tells the story of Shaver logging history and a bit of the SCE philosophy. Those who appreciate the beauty of Shaver Lake will enjoy reading Mr. Mount's comments.

The remainder of this section is comprised of a number of hikes in and around Shaver Lake. At the time of this printing, the trail that circumnavigates the lake was not complete. However, I anticipate that the day this book leaves the print shop, we will have a completed project! But don't let this book's inadequacies stop you. The twenty-four miles of shoreline beckon, and the intrepid will find their way. Just stick to the paths, and mind the signs marking the sanctuary for our rare, nesting bald eagles. Believe the biologist Steve Bird when he says you do not want to be anywhere near that nest when there are fledglings aboard. Those eagles get bigger and bigger as they swoop toward your head!

INTERVIEW WITH JOHN MOUNT

The most interesting story that I like to tell about Shaver lands is how they fit into the entire development of public lands and forested lands of the United States. You mentioned the East Coast being cut; it was actually cut by 1700, the New England states, and by the 1870s, Pennsylvania and Michigan had been entirely logged over. Everything was cut. The Southeast was pretty well cut. Our nation was looking for the next area to supply wood fiber for the growing nation and, of course, they looked to the West. There was great difficulty because how would you get the wood from the West to the East. The Transcontinental Railroad satisfied a part of that. Shipping, of course, still existed. The difficulty in the West was that there was no infrastructure: roads, canals (they did not have canals like the East Coast), rivers to float lumber down from the Sierras. Even the Northwest did not have the transportation means that the East Coast did. So that was the great hurdle that presented itself to the lumbering tycoons from the East Coast.

In the 1880's, a Mr. Long, the Long Family actually, developed a huge amount of interest in the Michigan area and that was where they were from. They had this young man who was willing to go west and stake a claim in the California area. His name was Charles Burr Shaver. C. B. Shaver, through some means, knew about the Shaver Lake area (of course at that time it was not called Shaver Lake). That was before Eastwood did any developing but had surveyed the area, so I am sure there was some tie-in from what Eastwood knew and C. B. Shaver knew. About 1890, Mr. Shaver and the Long interest, along with some of the other families, Swift, Forkner, and others in the Fresno area, decided they could build a dam for a millpond and a flume that traveled to Clovis and start logging off in the same manner that Pennsylvania and Michigan had been logged and the New England states. The lands were patented under the old Timber and Stone Act, which said that if you developed lands you could clerk at those lands and retain ownership. That was Congress' way of saying let's develop the West. They had the Swamp Act, the Homestead Act, the Timber and Stone Act, and several other Acts that allowed private individuals to take public lands for their benefit, but supply some kinds of goods and services to a growing economy and growing nation. That is what they did.

They built the flume. It was built by mills down the line, all along with other names that we know. Ockenden, Armstrong, and Cressman all built mills up and down the line and they were the ones that supplied the lumber for the flume. In 1892 this

24

operation started harvesting. They only took what was valuable to them at the time. What I mean by valuable was what was of value to them at that time. We think of them as being destructive, being bad land managers, when, in fact, they only took what would sell on the open market. They were not about to cut any trees just because they wanted to cut trees. No logger cuts a tree to cut a tree. Loggers cut trees so they can make money. The money is made because the consumers of the United States wants a particular product. That is how this area was logged. What made the Shaver Lake basin so valuable for this type of harvesting was there were so many trees that met their requirements of clear lumber. They proceeded to start harvesting along with several other mills in the area. The history Bert Hurt put together for the Forestry Service outlines all of the mills. Of course, the biggest and most prominent one was the Shaver Mill. They logged 450 million board feet by 1914, which was their last year of logging. They shut down because the economy went sour for building products. It was the very beginning of what we knew to be the Depression of 1929, but it actually started in the teens for agricultural products nationwide. That is what shut the mill down.

The lands that were left could be defined as clear-cut. There was no such term or social practices at that time that actually would of said clear-cut. That term had not been invented, thought about, or anything else by 1915, at least in the Shaver Lake area. The area was not clear-cut and a lot of trees were left that were young, too small, or twisted, or did not meet their specifications that the consumer was demanding at the time. So there were a whole lot of young trees left and they reseeded themselves and that is why this land looks different than some of the areas on the East Coast, or those areas that were clear-cut. They were not out to get rid of everything; they were out to get what they needed. The results of our lands were that there was a lot of openings, a lot of brushy areas, a lot of what we call meadows today, but are not really meadows. A very fragmented forest, but a young forest.

Edison Company came along and purchased the lands in 1919 to build Shaver Lake. Pretty much there was no economic value on the timber in the Shaver Lake area in 1919. The economic value of the forests in that area was in the areas of the Ockendens and other private lands that are now being subdivided in Shaver Lake. A whole neat economy of shakes and shingles, grape stakes, and posts developed from what was left by the early logging. Especially on other private lands, but even on the Edison Company land there were great big old Cedars. Cedar and fir had no value in those days; it was only the pines that held any value in those days. A tremendous shake and shingle industry was built in the Shaver Lake area. Tremendous amounts of shakes and shingles, as stories are told, of piles of 100 foot by 100 foot by 40 foot high of shingles and shakes from the Bretz Brothers in the early 1920's, 30's, and 40's.

As on the East Coast where different markets developed and different logging took place over the years and that is what also happened here in Shaver Lake. The White Fir, which had no value at the turn of the Century, but along came the agricultural need for boxes and crates, and lo and behold, Shaver Lake White Fir proved to be the number one "slicer" stock available for the market. A huge industry developed and companies as Associated Box, then became General Box and then various names after that, but they were all box companies and Shaver Lake White Fir became world renowned. Books from all over the United States described how Shaver Lake White Fir was so good. They would cut, not saw, so there would be no loss of the wood. All the fruit, grape, and packing trays, and everything, for the most part, came from Shaver Lake in those early years of the 1920's and 30's, and especially the 1940's and 50's. The slicer mill on Maple Avenue still existed when I moved up here in 1961. They were still cutting White Fir and it had become very valuable, even though it was low priced, which allowed the makeup of the forest to change from all White Fir and Cedar, and then allow foresters like myself to go out and harvest White Fir in the 1960's through the 1990's on Shaver Lake lands because those species of trees were left by the early loggers. The early history of the logging set the stage for how we manage our lands today here at the Edison Company. It is pretty neat. Knowing that history, knowing the natural history of the area prior to any European interference with our natural resources, and combining those two pieces of knowledge now allows me to rebuild the forest back into its natural state and at the same time continuing to harvest to pay for that rebuilding. That is why our forests look like they do today. We have been clearing brush fields and reforesting those brush fields. There were twenty-two donkey engines that worked on Shaver Lake lands, Edison Company lands, every day through the years of 1892 to 1914. Each one of them had a fire inside and the chances of starting a wildfire during those years were very high. I am sure that is what happened and when Edison Company started their forestry program in 1950. Large areas of brush still existed and when the first forester, Bill Wingo, started clearing and planting trees. So now we have several thousand acres of plantation trees.

Knowing that early history and knowing how the natural reproduction and flow of natural resources in the Shaver Lake area, I am now able to utilize that bit of knowledge in converting our forests. We use a "single tree selection." That does not mean that we don't cut two trees next to each other, it means we evaluate each tree individually as to whether it should be marked. Actually we do not evaluate the tree, but the stand that surrounds a particular tree, and we take those trees that will not only provide economic income but will leave the remaining, or residual forest, in the shape that we want. We want a fragmented forest. We want clumps of too dense of trees, we want openings, we want large trees and small trees, we want all species; so, by evaluating our forests and deciding which trees can be taken so that the residual trees will do the things that we want is what we call "Single Tree Selection." We are not just going out and deciding that we want a tree and taking it. What we really are doing is coming through the back door and seeing what we want the forest to look like, and then taking those trees that will allow us to maintain the forest. We have to look at all kinds of things: genetics, species mix, size class mixes, opening, ripening areas, meadows, and streams. All of those things as well as habitat trees that may be more valuable for habitat than others. Some trees that would be highly valued as lumber we leave and we put a "W" on them because they happen to have some attributes for wildlife. Other cases, we will do just the opposite. We will leave some scraggly old tree because it looks terrible because it may also have habitat or wildlife value. It is single tree selection, but we look at the stand as a whole. In the Sierra Nevada's, what we call clear cutting, patch cutting, or group selection, does not work if you open up an area because of the long dry summers we have here in the Sierras. The clear cutting in other areas may be necessary for those species type. I don't ever want to confuse those two facts. The boil forest requires clear cutting because if you do not open up a large enough area for the sun to hit, just the opposite as here, you have permafrost and it freezes over with a little bit of shade, and if you do not clear cut it the right species will not come back. The tundra areas require actual clear cutting. Just to compare this area to other areas would not be fair, but, on the other hand, the move to clear cut in this area was a travesty and that is why I am opposed to clear cutting in this area and developed the single tree selection.

Multiple Use Concept Of This Land

The term multiple use was actually used by the Forest Service in the 1960s. It was more political at the time and foresters had a very difficult struggle with it. Originally, multiple use was if you take one million acres and draw lines around certain areas of that one million acres, say Huntington Lake, and then say this area is for recreation use. You draw lines around other areas and say that this is for timber production. What we have demonstrated beyond a shadow of a doubt on Edison lands is that multiple use means multiple use on every single acre coincidentally. That is a huge difference from the original term of multiple use. We feel that every single acre can be used for every single use almost every year. The only time when certain areas are only used for certain things is during the birthing period for the wildlife. For example, our nesting pair of bald eagles. Around that tree, and indeed the whole ridge that nest tree exists, we do not get near. We do not walk in that area and don't want people to walk in that area because it disturbs the bald eagles greatly. Anybody that has walked near or under the tree knows how that bird will attack you and fly by you. That is the only time that we don't allow all uses on every acre, otherwise, even in Camp Edison it is a timber harvest area under certain conditions. We have to harvest trees in Camp Edison or pretty soon trees start falling over and limbs and hurting the campers. We have to manage the timber even in Camp Edison. We obviously manage the timber in Camp Edison differently than we manage around the bald eagle's nest. But we harvest timber around the eagle's nest and around the spotted owl's nest and then we leave it alone the way I described during nesting periods. But every single acre is open to hunting and bike riding. We reduce some uses like vehicle use because people just want to drive around and that causes disturbances. We have demonstrated through our selection cutting and our open door policy with very minimal and subtle restrictions that every single acre is used by every species of wildlife, including human wildlife. That is true multiple use. The resistance was felt in the past that you could not timber harvest an area and then the public would not accept it and would not go in there. It was thought to be incompatible to log and then have public use and that is not true as we have demonstrated. We burn, set fire to the forest, on purpose for certain attributes and the people come in afterwards mainly because that is when the deer come in and the deer hunters go into the area.

What do you see for the future of Shaver Lake?

What I foresee, the problems we had in 2001 with the State take-over and the high visibility of these lands and the unbelievable community public support to retain ownership by a private land owner thought to be bad in most circles of the United States demonstrated that people do understand the difference between good management and bad management and don't believe the only forest manager can be a government entity. Using that as an example, the example will exist for very many years. Our land management plan is firmly in place and I see our forest getting much better. Our goal is by the year 2033 our lands will almost exactly duplicate every single function that was found here pre-European time. Obviously on a different level of cycling because a natural time cycle would take five or six hundred years and we will reduce that down to two hundred or one hundred years. We will have larger trees, as many trees, and the right species of trees and we will have tremendous public support for that. We are thinking in our land management plan, our so called development plans of the west side of Shaver Lake, we are thinking one hundred years in advance. The love of keeping things natural will not go away. We could have wars that demand that we start logging our natural resources to support the war effort or something could happen where we would need large amounts of wood, this land could respond to that without hampering because the public still wants the natural resources. We would not hamper the natural resources and still provide the commodities that we need.

The cycles of economic well being, recessions, depressions will exist and it won't affect these lands in the long run. These lands are pretty much in shape even now, but will be in better shape in 2033 to absorb the cycles of wanting more trees cut or less trees cut.

That was my goal to put that kind of program in place where one year you could cut a little more and the next year a little less; twenty years cut a whole lot more or a whole lot less, and not affect the wildlife portion or the water cycles or other attributes of these lands. I am pretty optimistic that this will set the stage for the future of forest management.

On the lake we have approximately 570 thousand visitor days of use and don't know how much in the other uses. We are rapidly approaching one million visitors day use on our Edison lands. We only keep records on the lake use. The use of Shaver Lake could quadruple before any serious planning has to be done other than the subtle planning we are doing today.

The community itself is really a cross of people. We have people that want to leave the forest alone, they want nature there, yet are 100% behind the harvesting because they have come to realize that is what pays the taxes and keeps the land going. Even the most ardent nature lovers are my lookouts and let me know if something is amiss. They would really like the land left alone but see that the land can co-exist with the harvesting.

HIKE NUMBER 1
Granite Ridge Trail

Category: Easy
Length: 1.5 Miles Round trip
Time: 1 Hour
Map: U.S. G. S. Shaver Lake Quadrangle

Directions From Shaver Lake

From the hardware store in the center of the village of Shaver Lake, drive west (toward Fresno) 1.0 mile and turn left on Bretz (Mill) Road. Follow the road 0.7 miles to the entrance to the Granite Ridge subdivision.

Parking

Parking is available at the base of the entrance to the Granite Ridge subdivision. Be careful not to block either the access road or the entrance to the subdivision.

General Description

This trail is a contribution of the Granite Ridge subdivision to the recreational interest of the community. This lovely trail affords some excellent walking well within foot commuting access from Ockenden Ranch, the Bretz Mill Condominiums, and Sierra Cedars. The walk features an abundance of wildflowers, deer tracks, and bird watching. In addition to over 1.5 miles of great walking one can enjoy, the houses that you will see along the walk add to the excitement for the architectural esthetician. Since this trail's description was written, several miles of trail have been added by the Granite Ridge Association. Although not described in this edition, these trails are well marked, and the additions are easily negotiated. Thank you, Granite Ridge!

The Route

This circular route gives you the option of going either way around the loop. We prefer the counter-clockwise track for no particular reason!

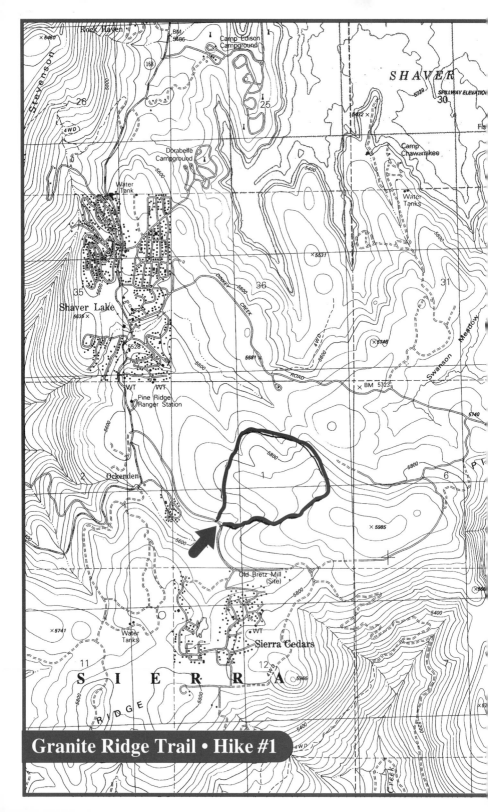

Granite Ridge Trail • Hike #1

Start on the right side of the entrance to the development. Follow the woods road uphill for .1 mile and veer right on to the path. This trail is marked with white "T" blazes and they will begin to be apparent as you make the turn onto the trail. Passing a picturesque rock outcrop (0.27 miles), the trail splits. Follow the right fork and walk 100 feet to the T shaped intersection on the exposed ledge. Turn right, walk up to the ledge and then left along the lovely ledge. After the trail traverses the ledge, it veers right leading one between a log house and the green water tanks that serve the community. The trail then crosses the road (0.4 miles) and continues toward the National Forest boundary (0.5 miles). Turning left, the trail descends beneath the shadow of some spectacular "cabins." The trail meets a dirt road (0.8 miles) and crosses to climb briefly before it traverses a meadow. Wending its way for the next 0.7 miles, the trail rejoins the entrance to the development and your starting point (1.5 miles).

Cautions

I am at a loss to think of any. Sure, you could see a snake, but as easily, a butterfly. As usual, vigilance is a good rule. However, this trail is a relatively safe, circuitous ramble through some lovely, local terrain.

Special Attractions

I like this trail because I can reach it from my house on foot. Not having to get in the car to go for a walk is very appealing. This walk has all of the charms of a wilderness walk, yet it is right outside my door in Ockenden Ranch. Oh, simplicity!

Driftwood Art by Tim at Shaver Lake

HIKE NUMBER 2
Shaver Lake Bridle Path

Category: Easy
Length: 2.5 Miles Round Trip
Time: 1 Hour
Maps: U.S.G.S. Shaver Lake and Musick Mountain Quadrangles

Directions from Shaver Lake
From the hardware store in the middle of downtown Shaver Lake, drive 1.2 miles northeast to the entrance to Camp Edison.

Parking
Parking is available within the confines of the campground for a small fee, or you may park just outside the grounds on Route 168. Be careful not to block the entrance to the campground or to obstruct the view of the sign.

General Description
This walk provides a lovely stroll through the woods adjacent Shaver Lake. Principally following the horse trails from the Shaver Stables, the Bridle Path features beautiful trees, spring flowers, and lake vistas. Commencing just a mile from town, the walk will please you with its natural beauty. In this area, I have seen coyote, deer, and birds. You can also discover quiet lakeside coves perfect for picnics or just a leisurely stop.

The Route
Begin at the intersection of the horse trail (the Bridle Path) and the entrance to Camp Edison. Turn left at the trail sign and proceed parallel to Route 168 through a beautiful stand of white fir and pine.

Passing a low, wet spot, rise up to meet a wood's road (.2 mile) and bear left to a telephone pole marked with a green hiker tag. Follow the road under the power poles approximately 100 yards and turn left off the road.

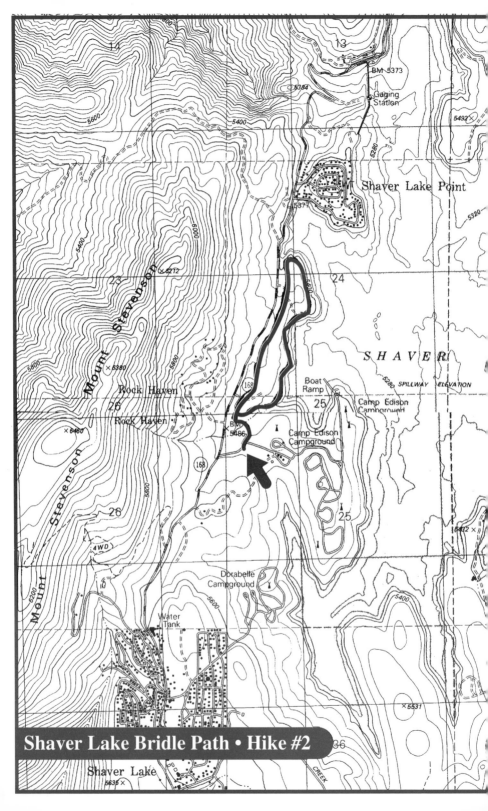

Shaver Lake Bridle Path • Hike #2

This jog is made to avoid the low boggy area you can see just ahead.

The trail rejoins the wood's road and leads directly on to the Shaver Stables' parking lot (0.5 miles). Walk straight across the parking lot, hop over a small stream, and gain the hill on the other side. The observant will find a small cairn on their right at the start of the hill. Rejoining the wood's road, bear left toward Bikini Cove.

As you approach Bikini Cove, you will encounter a group of roads. Keep to the Bridle Path and in a few yards you will find a sign indicating Bikini Cove is just ahead (1.1 miles).

At the cove, the trail turns right and follows the lakeshore back toward your start. Soon leaving the shady wood, the trail enters a manzanita grove with great views of the lake and Bald Mountain in the background.

The trail then bends around through the woods and descends to a point revealing Camp Edison's marina. This area is known as Rockhaven Cove. From here the trail continues around the cove to another beach front and picnic area. Here, the trial turns right and follows a road briefly before turning left and continuing the bridal path. This section winds through some beautiful shorefront before rejoining the wood's road and leading into the large meadow adjacent the Shaver Stables. Bearing left, a horse trail takes you to the power pole road. After this the trail on your right is rejoined and the path toward the start is revisited. Shortly, the Edison Camp road is reached (2.5 miles), and the walk is complete.

Cautions

Because you share the Bridle Path with the horses it was built to convey, you'd best look out for those beautiful beasts! Courtesy and safety dictate that walkers stand still and off to the side of the trail on the approach of horses. This move lessens the horses' anxiety about seeing such strange beasts as us. Additionally, if you have a dog, be sure to control (leash?) rover's excitement, too. Another caution is that this trial is not always obvious. Because of the many roads and horse trails, you will be given numerous choices. Don't fear or despair! You cannot get lost in this narrowly defined wood. The clear bounds of the road on one side and the lake on the other make for some distinct borders. You can always return on the road, or along the lakeshore. This is really a nice place to 'get lost'.

Special Attractions
There are lots of beautiful, natural attractions on this walk. Trees, flowers, and animals exist in their natural state beside the serene shoreline of Shaver Lake. The area also features examples of the Southern California Edison Company's excellent timber stand improvement and land management techniques. If you desire a short walk in close proximity to town, this trail is one of the finest!

HIKE NUMBER 3
Museum Trail

Category: Easy
Length: 1.1 Miles Round Trip
Time: 40 Minutes
Map: U. S. G. S. Shaver Quadrangle

Directions From Shaver Lake
From the hardware store in the center of the village of Shaver Lake, heading northeast, take your first right on Dorabella Road. Follow Dorabella Road to the U. S. Forest Service Campground at the lakeshore.

Parking
After paying your $3.00 entrance fee, you will find plentiful and safe parking a short distance down the hill from the gatehouse. The admission fee is well worth the investment!

General Description
This lovely walk links Southern California Edison Company's Camp Edison and the Dorabelle Campground with a one-mile trek through some well- managed woodland. A feature of this hike is the site of the Central Sierra Historical Society's Historical Museum site and a great variety of geologic, botanical, and horticultural items of interest. The museum is scheduled to be constructed in the year 2004. If we have another recession, it may be built in 3004! On our late August walk we sighted asters, mallow, vetch, monkey flowers, and bear clover to name just a sampling. The walk also features granite outcrops, glacial erratics and examples of exfoliation. Quite a nice slice of Shaver shorefront!

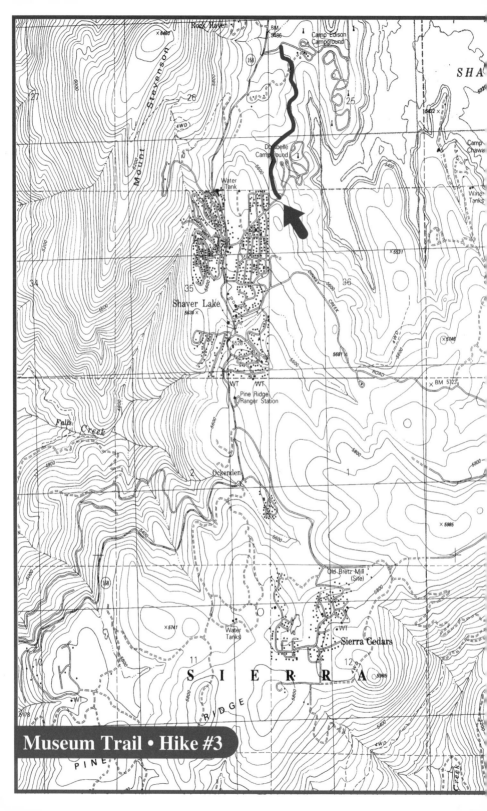

Museum Trail • Hike #3

The Route

Retracing your steps back up the hill from the gatehouse, you will soon meet the intersection of the trail and the paved road. Turn right and follow this well grooved horse trail toward Camp Edison. Hiking up a small hill, the trail breaks out onto an open ledge with views back toward Bald Mountain. Continuing under some power lines, the trail soon enters an area of aromatic bear clover. Following along the ridge, the trail enters an area of managed burn. These managed burns simulate actual fires and remove the forest floor's fuel source. This can prevent major damage during actual fires.

The trail then descends to a beautiful meadow filled with wildflowers. The meadow also features a stream. Ascending to an open ledge, examples of exfoliation and glacial activity abound.

At 0.66 miles, the trail meets a woods road and turns left. If you glance upward, you will see the windsock of the local helipad. Proceeding further down the road, turn left at the trail marker (0.8 miles) and head up a small hill. In another 0.1 mile you will pass the site of the Central Sierra Historical Society's museum. Winding along the trail, the paved access road to Camp Edison is reached at 1.1 miles.

Cautions

Not too many! Stay off the trail on the approach of horses and try not to trip on any roots while you are gasping at the beauty of the nature around you!

Special Attractions

The museum site and related items of interest are special! However, I also like the availability of a swim at the end of the hike back to Dorabelle Cove. The hotter the day, the more you will agree that a hike and a swim are a great combination!

Indian Acorn Grinding Holes

Carrie & Tyler on Shaver Lake

HIKE NUMBER 4
Dorabelle Cove

Category: Easy
Length: 2.8 Miles Round Trip
Time: 2 Hours
Map: U.S.G.S. Shaver Lake Quadrangle

Directions From Shaver Lake
From the hardware store in the center of the village of Shaver Lake, head northeast and immediately turn right onto Dorabella Road. Follow the road to its end at the U. S. Forest Service campground. Pay the $3 entrance fee and remember that you are contributing to the employment of the gatekeeper and all the other folks caring for the area. Don't you feel good? For comparison, therapy is $150.00 an hour!

Parking
This is why you just paid the three bucks! If you are the frugal type, you could park in town and walk to Dorabelle. But you're not! So enjoy the parking and the other amenities available for the dough!

General Description
This walk is a lovely, leisurely stroll along the southwest side of Dorabelle Cove. The trail crosses several meadows and has beautiful views of the lake below and beside you. A most pleasant perambulation!

The Route
Walking uphill from the gatehouse you remember so well, turn left off the Dorabella Road at the signpost at the trailhead. Head down the trail to an intersection at .2 miles. This left fork leads down toward the lake and rejoins the main trail (right) in the meadow ahead (.4 miles).
At .65 miles, you will reach a height of land and have nice views

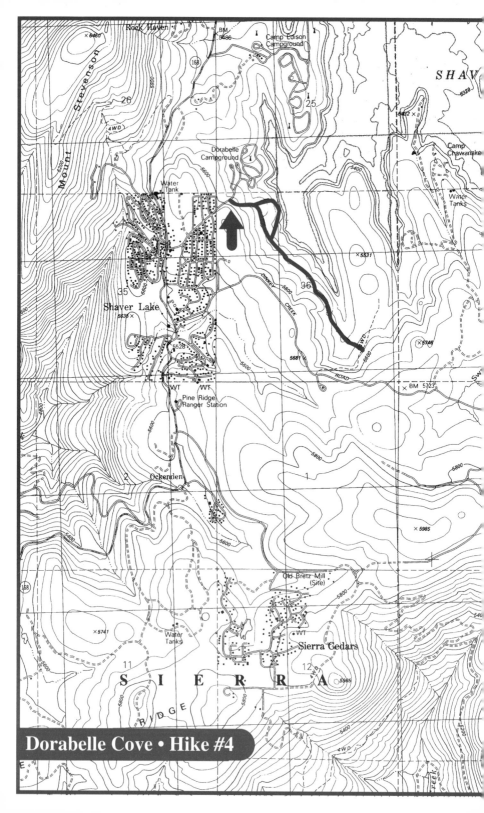

Dorabelle Cove • Hike #4

back down the cove. The mountain in the background is Stevenson Mountain. In another .1 mile the trail forks once again and you proceed to the right.

At .9 miles you will pass under the Meadow Way sign. This trail sign marks the cross-country ski trail. That is why the trail sign is posted so high upon the tree. At this point, slab right up away from the lake.

Just over one mile from the start you will pass a second Meadow Way sign. Continue along this trail until you meet the Nevin's Road trail at 1.4 miles. From this point the energetic can turn left and complete the Nevin's Road circle of about 2 miles. Others may prefer to simply turn around and retrace their steps back to the Dorabelle campground.

Cautions
This walk is maxed out on mellowness. Take care not to be lulled to sanguine lapses of merriment! As my friend Dwight Webb is fond of saying, "Too much of a good thing is wonderful!"

Special Attractions
Lake views and natural beauty abounds. The Southern California Edison Company has done a great job of managing the woodlands along the lake. This makes for a perfect habitat for birds and mammals. Southern California Edison Company's biologists have noted the presence of mountain lions on the point across Dorabelle Cove. If you are lucky, you will see a deer or an osprey.

Bob Penman, Trail Crew at Shaver Lake

HIKE NUMBER 5
Nevin's Road/Shaver Lake Shore Circle

Category: Easy
Length: 3-3.5 Miles Round Trip
Time: Approximately 2 Hours
Map: U.S.G.S. Shaver Lake Quadrangle
Special thanks to Jean and Lee Larson for maintaining this lovely walk.

Directions From Shaver Lake
From the junction of Route 168 and the Dinkey Creek Road, head east approximately 1.2 miles to the trailhead. Located on the left side of the road, the trailhead is directly across the road from the local landfill/disposal site. It is marked with a gate and a sign indicating "Nevins Road."

Parking
There is ample parking directly across the road from the trailhead. Take care not to block the entrances to either the Nevin's Road or the disposal site.

General Description
The Nevin's Road and the wood roads that connect to it provide a very lovely and leisurely walk. The trail ambles gently downhill to a well-marked series of woods roads that converge upon a shore adjacent to Dorabelle Cove. The walk features some of the excellent forest and land management practices that are employed by the Southern California Edison Company, such as selective cutting and replanting. The walk also features exciting bird and animal life. On our walk to the point, we observed a great blue heron and a red tailed hawk. Occasionally, osprey is also in flight looking for their prey!

The Route
From the Dinkey Creek Road, walk down the Nevin's Road .5

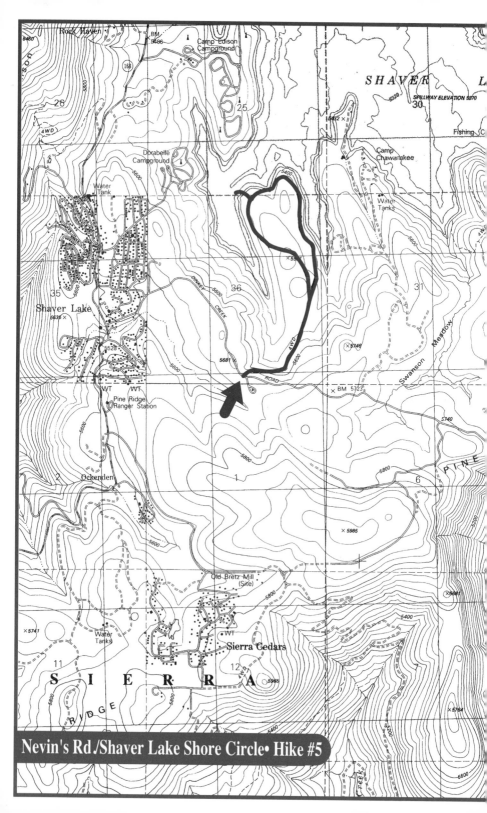

Nevin's Rd./Shaver Lake Shore Circle• Hike #5

miles to Landess Meadow. Walk past the trail marked "Inner Sanctum" and turn right onto Shorepoint Road (.66 miles).

This road passes through a gate (.9 miles) and overlooks the Boy Scouts of America Camp Chawanakee in the cove to your east. Follow Shorepoint Road to a junction (1.25 miles) and turn right (west). This path leads to its sandy conclusion at the lakeshore. From there we recommend a walk left to the end of the cove. This scant .5 mile is rich in wildlife.

Returning, follow the trail back to the Shorepoint Road and turn right. At the junction of the Inner Sanctum and the mid ridge road (1.82 miles), turn right on the Inner Sanctum. This route leads back to Nevin's Road (2.6 miles). Turning right (west), you will reconnect with your car in approximately .2 mile. All in all, one of the most peaceful walks in Shaver Lake!

Cautions

During hunting season you may encounter more excitement and activity than you would choose to include in your rambling! During this season, I prefer to roam the National Forest or head to the coast! But if you do walk during this time, wear a flame orange vest and hat and leave your buckskin jacket at home!

Special Attractions

Wildlife, birds, enlightened forest management techniques, and wildflowers are some of the highlights on the gorgeous, serene walk! Nevin's Road is the perfect place for a quiet picnic or a leisurely walk!

Tim, Andy, Mike & Jane taking a break
on Shaver Lake shore

HIKE NUMBER 6
Nevin's Road to Chawanakee Road Loop

Category: Easy
Length: 3 Miles Round Trip
Time: 90 minutes
Map: U.S.G.S. Shaver Lake Quadrangle

Directions from Shaver Lake
From Route 168, turn onto the Dinkey Creek Road and drive east toward Dinkey Creek for a distance of 1.2 miles. Turn right off the Dinkey Creek Road at the entrance to the landfill.

Parking
Parking is generally ample along the roadside. The trailhead is on the north side of the road and is marked with a large sign.

General Description
This is a pleasant hike through the woods. We describe it as a loop, but you can hike it any number of ways. You can plant a car at the Camp Chawanakee Road or simply retrace your steps. Any way you choose, the hike is most enjoyable.

The Route
From the trailhead on the Dinkey Creek Road, walk down the Nevin's Road 0.5 miles to Landess Meadow. Just past the meadow on the right, the trail to Burr Meadow turns off to the right. At this writing, there is a sign pointing the way.

Just a bit down the trail, two old outbuildings are still in evidence. This land was formerly the summer retreat of the Nevin's family from Clovis. The old fences and outbuildings were part of the camp they maintained on the property.

Follow the trail uphill until you enter a partially open area (0.9 miles). Turn left and cross a small streambed. Continue up to the height of land (1.0 mile). The trail then passes two side trails right and takes you up and over a final crest before dropping you into an

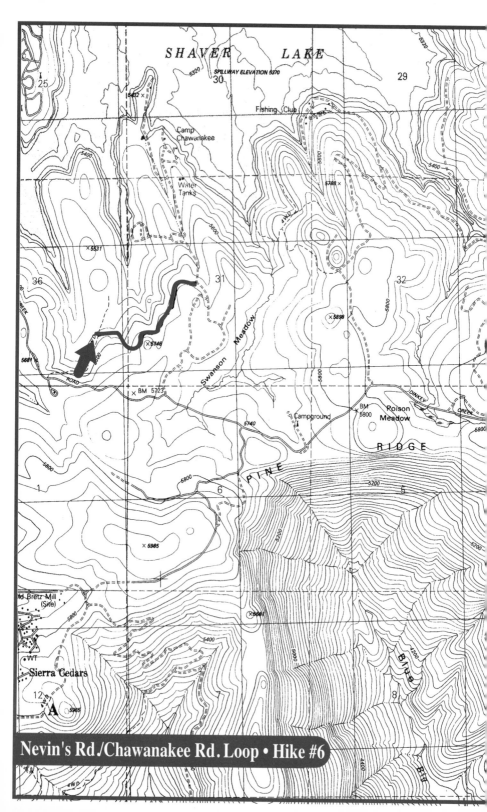

SHAVER LAKE

SPILLWAY ELEVATION 5370

Fishing Club

Camp Chawanakee

Water Tanks

Swanson Meadow

Campground

Poison Meadow

RIDGE

PINE

Bretz Mill (Site)

Sierra Cedars

A

Nevin's Rd./Chawanakee Rd. Loop • Hike #6

open area that leads out to the Chawanakee camp road (1.3 miles). At this point you can retrace your steps back to Nevin's Road, or you can follow our loop. Knowing your love of challenge and diversity, I imagine you taking the loop!

On the Chawanakee Road, turn right and walk approximately 0.7 miles to an abandoned road on your right. This road is marked by a barbed wire fence. (If you reach the Dinkey Creek road, you've gone too far. Retrace your steps 500 feet and the road will now be on your left!) On the wood's road, stay generally left and the obscure path will develop into a more substantial path in a short distance. When the trail appears more distinct, stay left. The trail eventually delivers you to the Nevin's Road just above Landess Meadow (2.5 miles). Turn left, and walk the last 0.5 mile up to the Dinkey Creek Road (3.0 miles).

Cautions
It is always a challenge to come up with a caution on a leisurely wood trek such as this. Please stay on the trail to avoid soil compaction unhealthy for the trees and do not remove any wildflowers or seed cones.

Special Attractions
This trail adds a nice compliment to the selection of trails that comprise the Shaver Lake basin trail system. If exploring is what you like, this adds a good three miles of new terrain for you!

Trail at Twin Lakes

HIKE NUMBER 7
Osprey Cove

Category: Easy
Length: 2.25 Miles Round Trip
Time: 90 minutes
Map: U.S.G.S. Shaver Lake Quadrangle

Special thanks to Rod and Marcia Weins for maintaining this lovely walk!

Directions from Shaver Lake
From Route 168, turn onto the Dinkey Creek Road and drive east toward Dinkey Creek for a distance of 1.8 miles. Turn left off the Dinkey Creek Road at the Camp Chawanakee sign. If the gate is locked, park to the side and walk on the dirt road 0.6 miles to the sign for the Pine Needle dump.

Parking
Parking is generally ample along the roadside.

General Description
The walk to Osprey Cove is a gentle, mile-long downhill rewarding the walker with a unique view of the lake. Our walk included four friends and three dogs! At the lake we were treated to an overhead flight of a bald eagle! We watched the eagle soar until an osprey arrived and sent the eagle on its way.

The cove was also covered with many deer tracks! A quiet day in the fall with hardly a boat on the lake, Shaver gave us a different look.

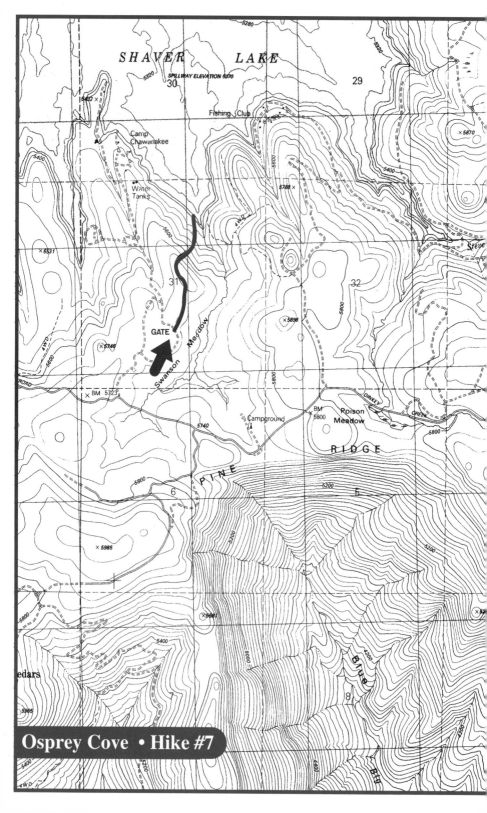

Osprey Cove • Hike #7

The Route

From the dirt road near the gate to the pine needle disposal, walk straight down the road and find a sign just behind an earthen berm. This sign marks the start of your walk. Follow the road past beautiful Burr Meadow and begin the gentle descent to toward the lake. At approximately 0.4 miles, a trail cuts off to the right toward Kokanee Point.

Farther along, the first views of the lake appear (0.8 miles). When you have walked just over a mile, you will come to a fork. The right fork will lead you to the lakeshore.

Cautions

It is always a challenge to come up with a caution on a leisurely wood trek such as this. Please stay on the trail to avoid soil compaction unhealthy for the trees, and do not remove any wildflowers or seed cones.

Special Attractions

For me it was that eagle, but I can't guarantee he or she will be there the next time. Why? Well, let's see. It could be that the pesky osprey had his way, or you might not be as lucky as we were. Yeah! That's it! But you will certainly find a lovely and isolated part of the lake. And the way the views are situated, the feeling is of being somewhere new and different!

Twin Lakes, the water is so inviting

HIKE NUMBER 8
Burr Meadow Road

Category: Easy
Length: 3.5 Miles Round Trip
Time: 2 hours
Map: U.S.G.S. Shaver Lake Quadrangle

Directions from Shaver Lake
From Route 168, turn right onto the Dinkey Creek Road and drive east toward Dinkey Creek for a distance of 3.2 miles. Turn left off the Dinkey Creek Road at the entrance to the fishing club and the perimeter road.

Parking
Parking is generally ample near the entrance to the gun club. Take care not to block the entrance to the club. The perimeter road is on the north side of the road and is marked with a large sign.

General Description
This is another pleasant hike through the woods on the road system that comprises the perimeter access to Shaver Lake. We describe it as a round trip walk hike in to the pine needle disposal, but you can hike it any number of ways. You can plant a second car at the pine needle dump just off the Camp Chawanakee Road or simply retrace your steps. Any way you choose, the hike is most enjoyable. Special thanks to Charlie Fergusson for discovering and describing this walk.

The Route
From the trailhead on the Dinkey Creek Road, walk down the Perimeter Road approximately 0.5 miles to a large oak in a stand of mixed soft and hard woods. The area is a good example of the selective cutting practices of the landowner, Southern California Edison.

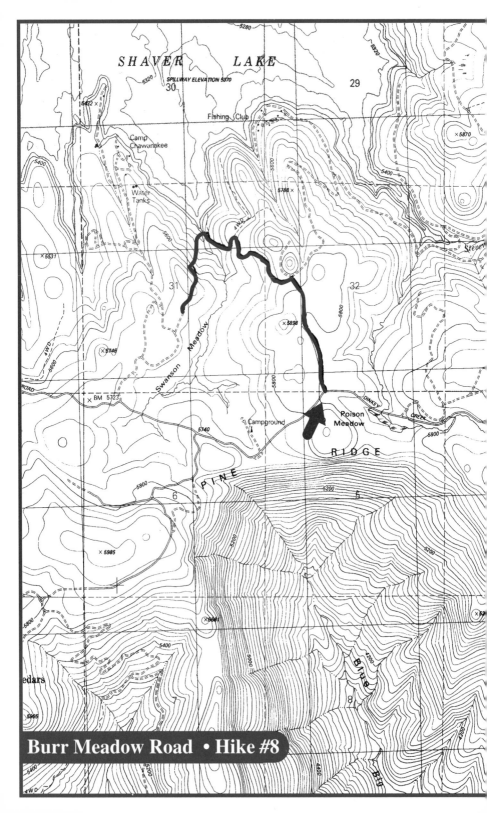

Burr Meadow Road • Hike #8

Shortly after this, the trail to Burr Meadow turns off to the left (0.6 miles). At this writing, there is a sign pointing the way.

Turn left, and shortly pass through a locked gate marking a "Wildlife Enhancement Area". At almost 1 mile, bear left as you approach a clearing. Shortly, stay to the right just beyond a "Wildlife Mitigation Area" sign. You will leave the meadow to your left. Follow along the base of a ledge, keeping it to your right.

Cross a stream (1.2 miles), and stay right at a fork entering a pine stand. Turn left at the next junction and shortly come to the Weins' Trail sign. This marks the pine needle disposal and the end of your walk.

Cautions
It is always a challenge to come up with a caution on a leisurely wood trek such as this. Please stay on the trail to avoid soil compaction unhealthy for the trees, and do not remove any wildflowers or seed cones.

Special Attractions
Again, this trail adds a nice compliment to the selection of trails that comprise the Shaver Lake basin trail system. If exploring is what you like, this adds a three and a half miles of new terrain for you!

Mike & Jane on the Shaver Lake beach

HIKE NUMBER 9
Fishing Club Road

Category: Easy
Length: 3.5 Miles Round Trip
Time: 2 hours
Map: U.S.G.S. Shaver Lake Quadrangle

Directions from Shaver Lake

From Route 168, turn right onto the Dinkey Creek Road and drive east toward Dinkey Creek for a distance of 3.2 miles. Turn left off the Dinkey Creek Road at the entrance to the fishing club and the perimeter road.

Parking

Parking is generally ample near the entrance to the gun club. Take care not to block the entrance to the club. The perimeter road is on the north side of the road and is marked with a large sign.

General Description

This is another pleasant hike through the woods on the road system that comprises the perimeter access to Shaver Lake. We describe it as a straight hike in to the fishing club gate, but you can hike it any number of ways. You can plant a second car at the Camp Chawanakee Road or simply retrace your steps. Any way you choose, the hike is most enjoyable.

The Route

From the trailhead on the Dinkey Creek Road, walk down the Perimeter Road approximately 0.5 miles to a large oak in a stand of mixed soft and hard woods. The area is a good example of the selective cutting practices of the landowner, Southern California Edison. Shortly after this, the trail to Burr Meadow turns off to the left (0.6 miles).

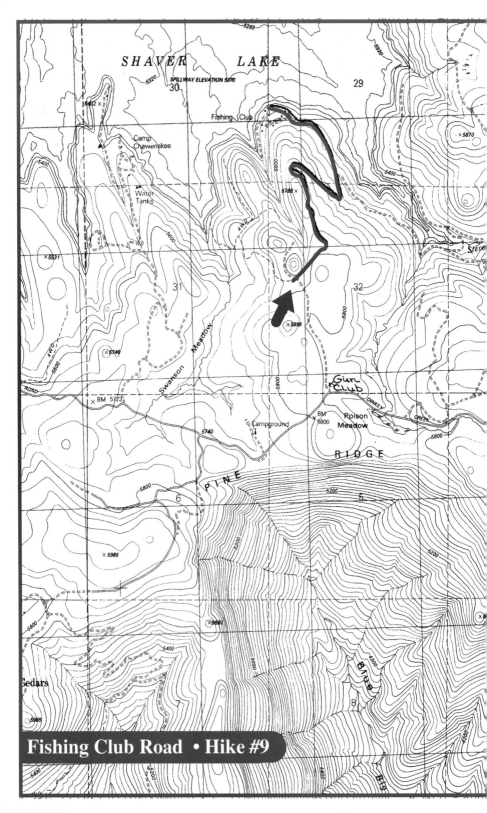

Fishing Club Road • Hike #9

At this writing, there is a sign pointing the way.

Continuing along the road, a logging road departs to the right (0.9 miles) as you turn left and proceed downhill toward the fishing club gate. At 1.75 miles, the road turns sharply right and the gate to the fishing club is directly ahead.

Cautions

It is always a challenge to come up with a caution on a leisurely wood trek such as this. Please stay on the trail to avoid soil compaction unhealthy for the trees, and do not remove any wildflowers or seed cones.

Special Attractions

This trail adds a nice compliment to the selection of trails that comprise the Shaver Lake basin trail system. If exploring is what you like, this adds a three and a half miles of new terrain for you!

Andy, Greg & Pearl on the Dogwood Trail,
Shaver Lake

HIKE NUMBER 10
Lake View Trail

Category: Moderate
Length: 9.4 Miles Round Trip
Time: 5 Hours
Map: U.S.G.S. Musick Mountain Quadrangle

Special thanks to Rich and Joy Bagley for assistance with this trail's maintenance and description.

Directions from Shaver Lake

From the hardware store in the middle of the village of Shaver Lake, drive North on Highway 168 4.0 miles to the entrance to the Shaver Lake Marina. Follow the entrance road left into the large parking area. You may park there or, if the gate is open, you can drive one mile further to a parking spot near the entrance to road three. Just past this point is a locked gate. The reason for the gate is that Edison lands are open to foot traffic, bicycles, and other non-motorized travel.

Parking

There is ample parking at the marina. At this location there is also a well-maintained toilet, picnic table, and shore area for play. Farther on, the parking is good, too.

General Description

This trail is a part of the Southern California Edison's Shaver Lake perimeter trails system, and it extends the perimeter road walk from Sulphur Meadow to the bridge crossing Tunnel Creek. This trail is most rewarding. It is well worth the time as you explore some lovely shoreline and professionally managed woodland. On our travels, Rich Bagley and I saw hundreds of wildflowers at the height of their bloom, and a great variety of birds were in evidence, too.

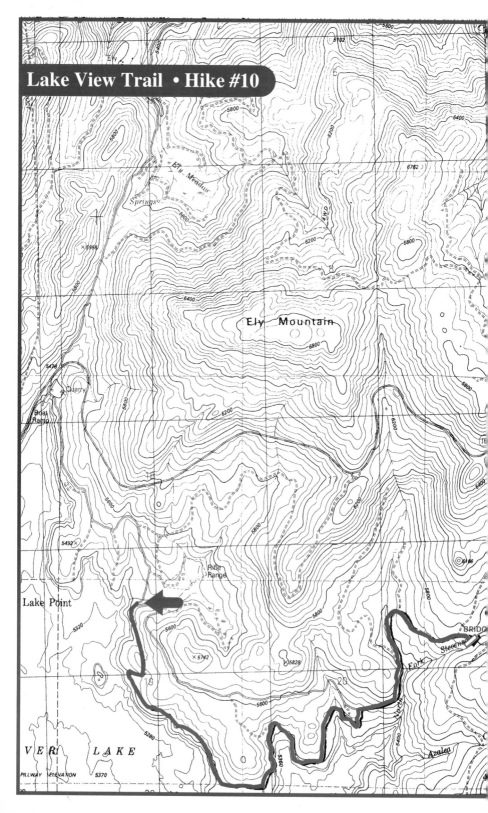

Lake View Trail • Hike #10

The Route

From the gate near the marine, follow the perimeter road to a locked gate (.9 miles). Continue past the gate to the streambed marking the bottom of Sulphur Meadow (1.4 miles). At this turn of the road, follow the sign straight into the woods on the Lake View Trail.

The trail enters the woods and follows the lake revealing beautiful views of both the water and the forest about you. The forest is open as a result of a policy of controlled burning to replicate natural forest conditions.

Continuing to rise, the trail leads to an area of logging activity (landing) and reaches a granite outcrop in 1.9 miles. From this height, walks out onto the ledge reward the walker with fine lake views. Now turning downhill, the entrance to Dorabelle Cove is visible to the west. At 2.2 miles, a large granite outcrop appears on the right. Following this to the lake, a picnic or a swim could be enjoyed!

In a moment, the trail takes a "T." Taking the left, the paved road is re-joined. Turning right, the trail continues to a sign pointing the hiker to the left and down toward Eagle Point Road. At 2.7 miles, the road enters an opening with signs directing the hiker to the tailrace straight ahead. (Following the road to the right, the Eagle Point day use area is reached. This is a bit of a dead end. For small bladdered walkers, there are bathrooms here and, for the hungry, nice spots to picnic.)

From the Tailrace/Eagle Point junction, continue another .3 mile to the opening across from Eagle Point. Later, at 3.5 miles, the trail regains the paved road and a sign tells the walker to turn left to return to the marina (4.5 miles) or to go right to continue the Lake View Trail. Assuming you are going right, continue past the Tailrace Road (3.6 miles) and walk another one third of a mile to the first over look of Stevenson or Tunnel Creek (3.9 miles).

Just beyond the creek, a beautiful meadow is gained (4.2 miles). The Stevenson Meadow Project is of special environmental interest because of the methods used to reconstruct the meadow to mid-Sierrian type. Now alive with birds and other animal life, the meadow is worthy of its environmental award status!

In another 0.1 mile, bear left passing the paved, tunnel entrance road to the right. Shortly, the Section 16 Road goes off to the left and the hiker continues right through an open area past a horse crossing sign. In a flash, the bridge over Stevenson Creek is reached (4.7 miles). This is the end of the Lake View section of the perimeter trail.

Cautions
There are a few on this tame, though lengthy, walk. It is possible to wander off the trail, but because you are walking between paved road and the lake for most all of the way, you cannot go too far afield!

Special Attractions
Given the timing of nature and your schedule, this is a winner for wild flowers! The variety of flowers and their profuse distribution along the hillside truly intoxicate the walker. My guess for the best time of year would be mid-June through early July, but each year is different. Your adventure will be to find the best time for you!

HIKE NUMBER 11
Bald Mountain

Category: Moderate
Length: 5.2 Miles Round Trip
Time: 3-4 Hours
Map: U.S.G.S. Dinkey Creek Quadrangle

Directions From Shaver Lake
From the junction of Route 168 and the Dinkey Creek Road, turn right on the Dinkey Creek Road. Drive 7.8 miles to the height of land (6,533 feet) and look left for a sign that says, "Bald Mountain." This marks the start of your trip.

Parking
There is ample and safe parking on either side of the Dinkey Creek Road at the height of land that marks the start of your walk.

General Description
This was one of my first finds in Shaver Lake. Distinctive in its prominence, Bald Mountain practically invites you to climb up to its summit. From the top, you can see the lake and the lands surrounding Shaver Lake from the perspective of a fire watch! The remains of the tower that was used for just that purpose still stands, though the men and women that used to occupy it have moved their station to Musick Mountain.

Memorable about the first outing to Bald Mountain was the arrival and landing of a helicopter. This coincided perfectly with the arrival of my dog Whitney and me. Dust flew and the dog took off! After a minute or two the helicopter flew off and Whitney and I regained our peace and composure!

Bald Mountain is also distinguished as the only mountain in the Shaver Lake vicinity that has a year-round jeep trail. The route described here meets that trail about half way up the mountain. If you want to avoid the traffic, stop your hike at the height of land (1.0 miles) before the trail descends to meet the jeep road.

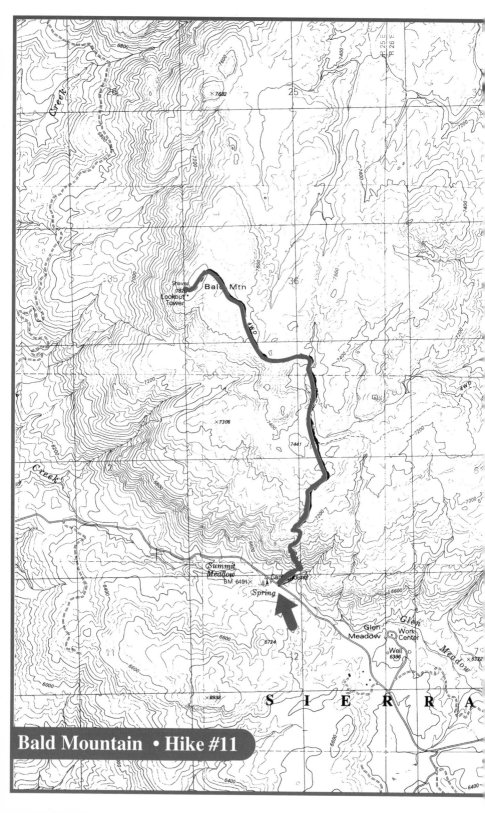

Bald Mountain • Hike #11

You still have some wonderful views of the Dinkey Creek Wilderness and the mountains to the east.

The Route

This trail begins just at the height of land, and it climbs quickly to great views (0.2 miles). Probably built as a quick ascent to the fire tower, this trail is not well suited for the faint hearted!

I've visited Bald Mountain many times and in a variety of conditions. This day, June 22, 1998, our group encountered snow that appeared to reach depths of eight feet! This added to the adventure and challenge!

Beginning at the road, follow the trail as it ascends through a beautiful pine and fir woods. Quickly, the trail begins to gain vistas to reward you for your hard work.

The trail is fairly well marked from previous walkers, and cairns are placed along the way. You will meet the first cairn at .6 miles. Because of the exfoliating granite, this is not a trail for sneakers. In fact, sneakers could be the equivalent of ice stakes on this slippery soil!

Reaching the top of the south face (1.0 miles), you will find spectacular views of the Dinkey Creek Wilderness and its characteristic Three Sisters. The Three Sisters are 10,000-foot mountains that buttress the many lakes that comprise the region.

Traveling on, the trail dips downward to deliver you to the junction of the jeep trail (1.2 miles). Turn left and follow along through the lodgepole forest. Don't be too shocked to find a cow or two grazing on the sweet grass in this area.

Coming out of the woods, the trail ascends to remind you of the aerobic value of hiking! Coming up and over the ridge, more beautiful views of Bald Mountain reward you. The trail then leads you closer to the fire tower is now visible for the first time.

Gaining the top (2.6 miles), you'll enjoy the great views of Shaver Lake and the surroundings. With any luck, you'll have the place to yourself. Given the possibility that you will be joining a jeep club for lunch, you may choose to eschew the summit. With a little creativity, you will easily find a private spot!

Cautions

One of the two cautions that stand out on this trip includes the slippery granite dust that covers some of the trail's steep spots. This makes hiking boots imperative. Bald Mountain is definitely not a sneaker trail! With small children, I would also recommend a rope in places. This trail has a couple of exposed pitches, and a slide could be injurious.

The other caution concerns the jeep trail. Most of my trips up Bald Mountain have been in isolation. This is part of the joy of the mountains for me. However, on occasion, I have been joined by seemingly unmuffled dirt bikes with riders in search of an audience! I hope your walk is more quite than that walk was for me!

Special Attractions

For the budding geologist, there is much to see in the way of exfoliating granite, weathering, and other features. The views are worthwhile, and this may be the best half-day hike in Shaver!

HIKE NUMBER 12
The Dogwood Trail

Category: Moderate
Length: 5.2 Miles One Way/10.4 Miles Round Trip
Time: 2.5-5 Hours
Map: U.S.G.S. Musick Mt. And Huntington Lake Quadrangles
Special thanks to Tim and Pam Geisel for creating and maintaining
this wonderful walk.

Directions from Shaver Lake
From the hardware store in the middle of the village of Shaver
Lake, drive north 4.2 miles to the turnoff for the Huntington Lake
Road. Continue 0.5 mile further to the height of land. The
trailhead is marked by a steel gate on your right.
To avoid retracing our steps, we spotted a car at the Balsam Fore-
bay snow park. Directions to the snow park are included in the
Balsam Forebay hike. The distance given for this hike is one way
from Mt. Ely to Balsam Forebay.

Parking
Parking is available just off the road by the gate. Take care not to
block the entrance to the gate, or you will get a note from the
gatekeepers reminding you of their need for access in case of fire
or other emergency.

General Description
This is a lovely walk with views of the back of Yosemite National
Park and Kaiser Peak. For most of its route, the hike clearly follows the Mount Ely road along the backside of the mountain. The
challenge begins where the road dissolves from lack of use and
your skill as a route finder is required. Where this problem arises
is accurately described. Perhaps by the time you read and walk
this trail, improvements will have been made to clarify the ambiguities. As of this writing, the middle of this walk is more closely a
deer and animal trail than a footpath.

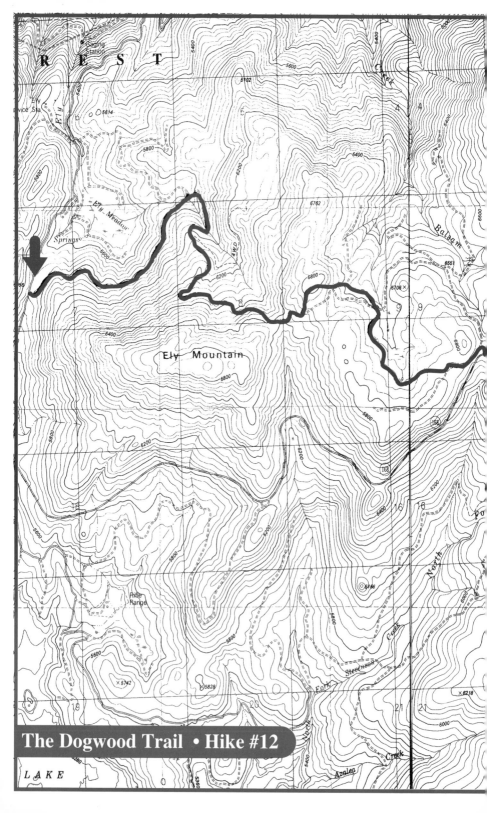

The Dogwood Trail • Hike #12

The Route

From the Huntington Lake Road, walk past the gate and the heliport in a generally northeast direction following the obvious power lines. The roadway is obvious, and continuing, you will find a beautiful view of Kaiser Peak. At this point (0.2 miles), enter past a gate marking Southern California Edison's wildlife enhancement area.

Continuing along the road's easy grade, you will find views of the backside of Yosemite National Park (0.4 miles). At this point the trail winds eastward, and the woods begin to change to predominantly fir and sugar pine.

At 1.3 miles, cross a large culvert, and an old meadow is revealed on your left. From this spot, hike up the road generally north-northeast. In a short distance (1.6 miles), you will re-cross the stream as the road turns west. Shortly after the stream crossing, enter an old yarding area. Yarding is a logging term for logging truck landing area. Turning southeast, the road continues giving a view of the low crag marking the site of Nellie Lake on the west side of Kaiser Peak.

Continuing on the road, signs marking Southern California Edison's wildlife mitigation area are prominent (2.0 miles). In a short distance, the road brings you to a good view of Musick Mountain as it turns sharply southeast. Here the grade moderates. At 2.7 miles, the road forks. Bear left and continue slightly downhill. In a few steps, more views of Yosemite open to the north-northeast.

At 3.1 miles, the road splits and the ambiguities begin. The road at this point dissolves and the only indications of its former presence are the water bars left to prevent erosion. From here, slab uphill in an easterly direction. This is a bush whack to the rocky out crops marking the top of the hill. Covered with black oaks, the hilltop (3.3 miles) makes a good spot for a stop.

After reaching the crest, turn right and generally east-northeast through a control burn area to meet a logging road. Follow the road to the right or south up and down passing some splendid glacial erratics (huge boulders left by the glacier). At 3.8 miles, pass a large microwave deflector (or is that a billboard for wild animals?) and continue to follow the road.

Shortly, you will meet the power line from powerhouse Number 2. Turn right and head east following the road underneath the power lines. At 4.2 miles, you will see the green fence guarding the quarry excavated to build the dam at Balsam Forebay. The fence is to protect unwary deer and other animals from discovering the steep sides of the quarry unexpectedly.

Here you may make a choice of routes to reach the snow park. The snow park lies on the opposite side of the forebay from where you stand. The simplest way back is to follow the road you are on. Hiking to the right or south, the road winds its way around the forebay and leaves you at your car. Total distance equals 5.2 miles. I prefer to follow the fence south and down toward the right to a locked gate. The gate is easily opened and the scramble down the scree slope to the bottom is fun. From the bottom, walk toward the forebay and turn left toward the dam (4.4 miles). Cross the dam and observe the Balsam Creek emanating from the base. This is the water supply for Camp Sierra.

Follow the road, and find an earthen/granite dam at 4.8 miles. Shortly afterwards (0.1 mile), the trail to the snow park cuts off to the left. Its entrance is a bit obscure, so if you pass the out houses on the right, you have gone too far. On the trail, the path is clear, and the snow park is reached in one half mile.

Cautions

This trail is obvious for the first three miles, but after that one must be prepared for a half mile of confusing bush whack. Without compass, map, and experience, this could be a poor choice. This is magnified if you are the leader, and your charges are even less prepared for the challenge.

The other caution is the steep scree slope near the forebay. This, too, is not a spot for those unaccustomed to ungroomed footpaths.

Special Attractions

Lots to see on this wonderful 5 mile excursion. Enjoy.

Greg at Rancheria Falls,
Huntington Lake

HIKE NUMBER 13
"72 Road Trail"

Category: Easy/Moderate
Length: 5.2 Miles Round Trip
Time: 2.5 Hours
Map: U.S.G.S. Musick Mt. Quadrangle

Directions from Shaver Lake
From the hardware store in the middle of downtown Shaver Lake, drive north 4.2 miles to the turn-off for Sierra Marina. Follow the road as it bears left around the lake. Go through the first gate and continue along until you reach a locked gate (a total of approximately five miles from the village).

Parking
At approximately 5.0 miles, look for a place to park on the side of the road. Parking is generally ample along the road. Do not block the gate.

General Description
This is a very mellow walk fit for any Spring-Fall half day. The walk follows the land's contours up to meet Route 168. Along the way, the hiker is rewarded with views of Shaver Lake, Bald Mountain, Mt. Ely, Musick Mountain, and Flume Peak. Our walk was adorned with a dusting of freshly fallen snow. This made for easy identification of the tracks of deer, raccoon, pine martin, and rabbit.

The Route
Just past the large, locked gate at 5.2 miles, the Lower 72 Road leaves left (5.3 miles) and heads east up the hill. The trail/road follows the hill upward through some of the Southern California Edison company's managed woodland. This woodland is managed for both sustained yield and fire prevention. Selectively thinning the forest is also advantageous for wildlife management.

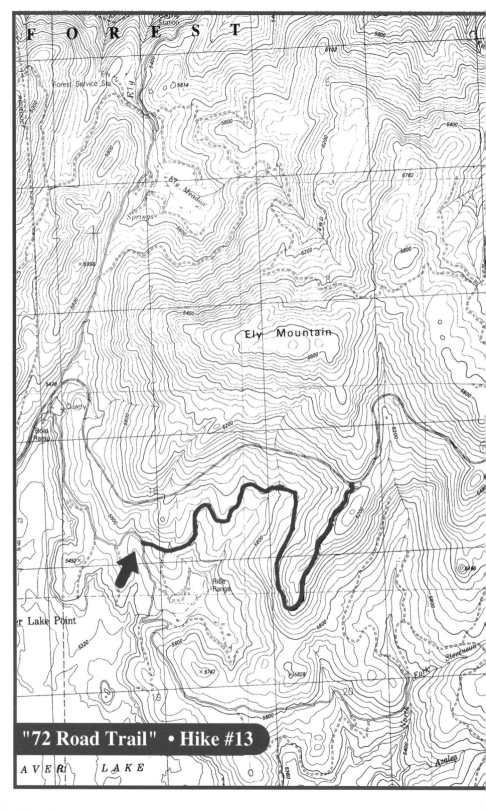

"72 Road Trail" • Hike #13

In 0.4 miles, an interesting boulder area appears on the left. Some of these boulders are glacial erratis. These are boulders carried by the glaciers of 10,000 years ago. These boulders were deposited when the glaciers receded. From the boulder area, the trail continues to snake its way upward. Further on the left, a tall, burnt skeleton of a cedar tree is evidence of the damage of fires past. At 0.57 miles, the road passes a large ledge on the left. From this outcrop of granite, black oak and pine spring out from the rock. This ledge is part of a series of ledge outcrops that continue to adorn the walk. At 1.2 miles, the trail passes a meadow and turns right (southeast). Further, at 1.6 miles, views of Musick Mountain and Ely Mountain are visible. Views of the lake, Bald Mountain, and other local landmarks characterize the rest of the walk. In a short distance, Route 168 is reached (2.6 miles).

The return trip simply involves retracing your steps to Highway 168. This concludes a wonderful walk by the lake.

Cautions

It is always a challenge to come up with a caution on a leisurely wood's road trek. I'm stumped!

Special Attractions

Seeing so many other hills and the lake make one happy to be a part of nature. This is a lovely walk perfect for a half days journey away from the TV and the phone. Be sure to leave yours in the car!

Doug & Chloe, A view atop Ely Mountain,
Shaver Lake

HIKE NUMBER 14
Ely Mountain

Category: Moderate
Length: 2.5 Miles Round Trip
Time: 3.0 Hours
Map: U.S.G.S. Musick Mt. Quadrangle
Special thanks to Doug Waugh and Chloe French for their good work in maintaining this trail.

Directions From Shaver Lake

From the hardware store in the middle of downtown Shaver Lake, drive north approximately 4.25 miles on Highway 168 to the Huntington Lake Road. Just after you pass the Shaver Lake Marina, turn left on the Huntington Lake Road and continue approximately 0.5 mile to the steel gate that bars the entrance to the heliport. This spot is at the top of the col (ridge) on the right hand side of the road.

Parking

Parking is available either uphill or downhill from the gate. Because this heliport is for emergency medical evacuations, please do not block its entrance.

General Description

Ely Mountain is easily the most exciting, spectacular, and convenient hike in the Shaver Lake area. Less than five miles from town, the mountain offers lovely views of Shaver Lake and a range of mountains from Yosemite to Kaiser Peak on the north.

The Route

From the steel gate at the road head, walk into the heliport entrance and proceed generally north along the logging road for a few minutes until you reach a second steel gate. Continue approximately 100 yards until you encounter the trailhead sign on your right and enter the clearly marked trail.

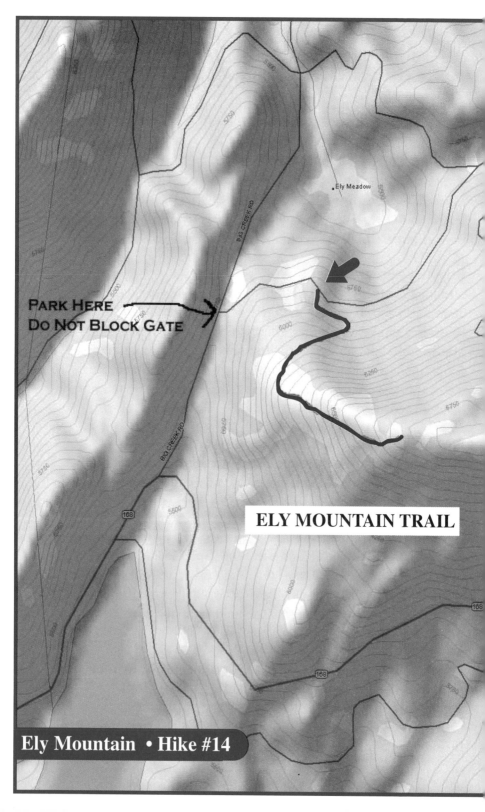

PARK HERE
DO NOT BLOCK GATE

. Ely Meadow

BIG CREEK RD

BIG CREEK RD

(168)

5500

ELY MOUNTAIN TRAIL

(168)

(168)

Ely Mountain • Hike #14

From the start the trail climbs steadily up the first of several pitches. During your ascent, enjoy the songbirds, manzanita and oak groves, and the lovely views of Kaiser Peak, the penstocks rising to Huntington Lake, and the clear Sierra skies. The trail meanders through the forest, rising and falling a bit, until you arrive at a large fallen tree, which provides a nice resting and viewing place.

Proceed on up the trail until the trail meets a dry streambed. Follow the streambed up for approximately 200 feet. Here the trail leaves the streambed to the right. A bit further on, the trail heads onto granite and begins to climb up the dome. Look carefully for the cairns, which can be hard to see against the rocky surface.

At the halfway point on the granite slab, "Pine Island" affords a nice respite and water stop. This is also a lovely place to stop to hear the screech of an osprey or red-tailed hawk, and the clacking of the raven or, if you are especially lucky, to watch a bald or golden eagle soar above you (yes, Shaver has both on its shores). As you follow the cairns up the granite, your view of Shaver Lake will increase until the final large cairn on top of the dome. The trail stops here, but you can bushwhack to the summit if you feel adventurous. From the end of the trail at the big cairn, you can see the summit of Mount Ely. The summit is approachable from either the left or the right. However, I prefer to ascend from the left and descend to the right. There is good bushwhacking up and down if one is careful to avoid the steep pitches in the middle of the mountain. The middle appears technical (requiring ropes) and could provide good friction pitches. The top is gained at 0.9 miles. Although not the true summit, the views from and the beauty of this spot surpass those of the actual summit, which is 0.5 mile further along the ridge to the east. Descent is made by following one's footsteps back down to the slab, or by forging ahead and looping around the summit. To loop around the summit, walk about 100 yards past the top and turn down towards the lake. Two hundred yards down the mountain, you will encounter a large glacial erratic (boulder). Walk below this boulder and bear right to return to the slab that marked your ascent. Descent form the big cairn is made by retracing one's footsteps back down the slab and the trail.

Cautions

In wet weather and when the snow is on the ground, this route should not be attempted. The steep pitches and the lichen-covered rock do not make for good footing. This trip is also not for the faint of heart. The ledge or slab is fairly exposed and the feeling of being "out there" may be a bit much for some of the less intrepid among us. As a mitigating factor for young children or the faint of heart, a climbing rope might provide the extra security needed to make this trip a go. Furthermore, the trail is marked only intermittently with cairns (rock piles) and ducks (rock stacks). If you lose the trail, return to the last known location and try to relocate from that point. The thick brush at the bottom of the mountain makes for a nightmarish bushwhack!

Special Attractions

The mountain features Wild Iris and Feather Peabush among the many flowers on display in season. Deer and bear tracks abound! The birding is also excellent, and the views are unparalleled! Doug Waugh waxed poetic in describing his experience of climbing this trail and sitting on the dome overlooking Shaver Lake: "a 'Zen-dorphin' high" We hope you will also get this euphoric, peaceful feeling when you reach the top!

THE HUNTINGTON LAKE REGION

The Huntington Lake region is unique because of its size, elevation, and proximity to the central Sierra. Located high in the mountains, Huntington Lake stays cool even on the hottest days of summer. This coolness also creates a draft that brings strong breezes each afternoon. For this reason, Huntington Lake is the site chosen for a series of sailing regattas that entertain boaters and spectators alike. The colorful spinnakers make the lake come alive after its white winter covering of snow and ice has disappeared. Many of the Valley's families have historically summered in the Huntington Lake region. The community has a rich history of summer events that have brought joy to the many who have had the opportunity to experience Huntington's hikes, fishing, or dances at Lakeshore. One of the families with a long history of experiences at Huntington is the Blasingames. For four generations, the Blasingames have come from the Valley to graze cattle in the meadows that surround Huntington Lake. Although the family no longer brings cattle to the area, the stories Knox Blasingame provides show some of the colorful history of this area.

Knox Blasingame: Story of the family coming to the foothills.

The Blasingames are not record keepers or diary keepers, as I don't think too many of them could write. The first one we can positively identify was our great, great grandfather, and he came from Alabama. This was northeast Alabama, and I believe it was hill country. And he had several sons. He had one or two sons that left Alabama when the Mexican-American War was taking place, which would put it in the 1840s. They joined in that, went to the Battle of Vera Cruz and then he came back, and they mustered him out in Texas. He and other members of his family stayed for about a year or so in Bell County, Texas, which is in the Waco area. Gold was then discovered in California so being normal young men, they thought it was exciting and off to California they came. There are two versions of how they came here. One was a wagon and the other was that they went back to the Gulf and took a boat down and walked across the Isthmus of Panama and caught another boat on the other side and ended up in San Francisco. The next records we have of them, they were registered as gamblers in the Mother Lode Country. This was in 1849 that they came to California. Then a couple of years later there was a census, and they were found to be registered as gamblers. Jesse Augustus Blasingame, Jr. was my great grandfather. He married Mary Jane Ogle, who had come from St. Louis in a wagon train. They settled in a little town called Vallecito in the Mother Lode. They started a family and had two boys while living in Vallecito. They had a store, living quarters, and places to gamble in a mine in the foothill country of the Mother Lode. The mine had a wooden structure at the entrance and then the mine went back into the mountain. One night after they closed the store, the father was counting the money and closing things up. As the wife looked up she sees a man crawling on the floor with a knife. She whips a gun out from behind a door and shoots the guy about the time he was attacking her husband. The shot kills him. He was a Native American that lived there, and they were concerned that someone would retaliate, so they packed up and moved to Auberry. This was in the latter part of the 1850s. The exact year I am not sure. They lived where the new grade runs into Lodge Road where the new highway starts and lived there for a couple of years. While living there they had two daughters who were born and who eventually died. The girls are buried, along with their father, in the old cemetery down near Roeding Park.

After that (not sure of the time frame) he moved to Academy, on Big Dry Creek. From the Mexican American War he was in, they paid him script when they mustered him out. They did not pay them much when they were in battle, but paid them at the end with script that could be exchanged for land that was acquired from the Mexican American War. He was able to change some of this script for ground here in California and that is how he got started. The gambling thing I don't know exactly how much he was into it, but there are a couple of stories. One of them was he was in Academy and raising hogs and sheep. Having been from the Mother Lode, there was not much market from the livestock he raised. He would drive the hogs from Academy all the way up into the Mother Lode country. Each town he came to he would sell a few hogs and then continue on to another town to sell. There were quite a few Chinese in those days, so the Chinese really liked the pork and that made a good market for it. On this one trip when he finished selling all his hogs, he was enticed, or might have even suggested it, into a card game. He did not do well and lost all his money. He, with the rest of the drovers, decided to come home. They arrived home a couple of days later and his wife was waiting for him. (I think she might have been a little spitfire.) She asks him where the money is, and he tells her he lost it in a card game. She goes into her stash to get more money to stake him in a game and said to go back up there and not to think about coming home until he got all his money back. He proceeded to do that and came back home in about ten days and was allowed to stay, so apparently he got his money back.

After they moved to Academy no one was into livestock, so one thing led to another. Then he got into the hogs, then sheep, and then eventually cattle. He had quite a large family, nine or ten children. He then came into town (H Street was the main street in Fresno in those days and everything faced the railroad track) and opened a hotel, called the Ogle House (after his wife's maiden name). It had something like 60 rooms and was fairly large. Knox remembers coming into town as a young child to that hotel. Eventually, it became old and was in the bad part of town so they tore it down and sold the lot. With all the children he had, some went into the livestock business. Several of them became vinyardists along with the livestock. There were all different personalities, too.

My grandfather, who was the youngest one of the bunch, had a pistol as a child. He had a shell that he was trying to put into the pistol and the shell was just a little too big for the chamber. He tried to tap it into the chamber, but it went off and shot him in the leg. It slowed up his life some because they never got the bullet out and it rubbed up and down on the bone a lot. He was not a healthy man at all. He eventually died just below Edison Lake in what we call China Camp. He had a heart attack and his son had to pack him out on horseback. Most of the male Blasingames were in the livestock business and kept going down the ranks in the family until there is not much more of it left today.

From the hog business to the sheep business, and I am sure they were overlapping a bit, at the time they were running the sheep, they ranged from as far as Kettleman City to south of the south fork of the San Joaquin, Rock Meadow and Red Mountain and that country. That is how China Peak got named. A Chinaman stayed up there with the cattle during the summers. Laconte was a friend of this old Chinaman, and he would visit whenever he was in the area. Through these visits and talking with him for several years, he named the mountain after him because that is where the old guy stayed.

After the Forest Service came into the picture and said they did not want any more sheep on the forestland but they would allow them to run cows instead of sheep. At that time, about 1900, they came to the family and told them if they would drop to Rock Meadow and Red Mountain area and go across to the south fork of the San Joaquin, they would allow them to make that trade and would be allowed to take 1,000 mother cows in there. At that time, the permit went up into Mono Creek and the starting of the recesses. It actually went from the Mono Crossing on Mono Creek (down where the 61 forebay is) and went across up Mono Creek a ways and clear over Silver Pass into what we call the Fish Creek area. Actually, Fish Creek itself was the extreme north boundary of the permit (very close to Mammoth Ski Resort), and it came from that clear down to Cassidy and towards Miller's Crossing. My dad acquired Sample Meadow and Kaiser Peak Meadow. He bought them from George Ship. He also got the Mt. Tom allotment, which was Sample Meadow, Huffman, Dalton, and all that kind of river slope country. When I was a teenager, my dad also got the Huntington Lake allotment with it. And that went down to Chawanakee, in below Big Creek. Our family was kind of in a phase. A lot of the older people in my dad's era were dropping out, and he was acquiring the land. This was just the beginning of the Depression. My dad, his father, and his uncle, Will Blasingame. Will starts to go broke because Will ventured out into things in Northern California and the banks were really after him, so they dissolve partnerships to salvage the rest of it. Some of his other uncles who had been in the livestock business are dying off. At this point, my dad was the only Blasingame going to the mountains with the cattle. My dad's mother was a Sample and they were also livestock people. After my grandfather died, my dad and his mother were partners for a number of years.

Way back in the beginning there was an old gentleman that came in with Fremont and ended up going back and forth a few times. He eventually married a lady by the name of Sweeney. He ended up in Academy and had eleven daughters. From these daughters, the oldest one married D. C. Sample (those were the parents of my dad's mother). At one time, about 90% of the people that ran livestock in the mountains between Kings River and Middle Fork of the San Joaquin were related. You could go every night and stay at a different relative's home if you wanted to take a trip through the mountains. But then they all began to die off and fade out.

In the 1940s, most of my dad's help were Native Americans, and they were all excellent cowboys. Times change and logging is paying a lot more and they are getting this government money for the Indians, that labor force begins to dwindle. It was kind of sad because these were really good guys and workers and pretty much got themselves into the main line of living just like Europeans demanded they live. Then all of a sudden comes out this free money and it really deteriorated for a number of years. It was really a tragedy for them.

As a general rule, the Native Americans were excellent cowboys. By the time I am old enough to remember them, there were very few 100% Native Americans, they were all intermingled to some degree. A lot of them you could not tell it, but they had Chinese in them. Now-a-days, if there is Chinese, you don't see it. Chinese came during the influx of the gold rush time and the railroad; probably the railroad as much as anything. There were several guys that worked for my dad that were part Chinese. Several of the Goode family had Chinese in them. Charlie Lee, he only had one child, so only made one there. Some of them could not read or write but they were wonderful guys. Honest as the day is long. Uncanny as far as cowboys. Not too many liked the young horses so much. This Greg Goode that I speak of, he was exceptional and would start with a lot of colts and rode a lot of colts and was very good with it. They did have idiosyncrasies. A lot of times, if you would be in camp for a long time together, sometimes you would be together constantly for a month or so at a time, and maybe one day you would get up and all the Indian boys were not talking any more. Never have any cross words, but they would go into these quiet spells that might last for a week or ten days, or it might last until you got out of the mountains and had a little change for a while and then they would talk great again. They talked enough to get their work done, but as far as having a conversation with them, they did not care about that.

My great grandparents were living in a two-story adobe house that was built by John Scheid in the very early 1850s. It was probably one of the oldest houses in Fresno County, and I don't think the Historical Society even knew it existed. They had quite a few children and their main source of supplies was either Stockton or San Francisco. They took some livestock to Stockton and told her husband that after he sold the livestock to go on to San Francisco and get some necessary supplies for the next year and also to bring back someone to help her in the house. He is up there and walking down the street in San Francisco and there is this little Chinese boy standing in the corner crying. He was maybe 10 or 11 years old. His parents were not anywhere around and the person he had been working for had abused him quite badly. He ends up coming home with my great grandfather and is going to be the houseboy. By the time the little boy arrives and goes with the cowboys a few times, he does not want much to do with the house. He became a live-stock man and stayed with the livestock as long as he lived there on the ranch. He was a very good livestock man and had this very fancy horse named Yellow Money that he was extremely proud of. He had Shepherd dogs that were suppose to be quite good.

He would go up into the mountains every summer as soon as the snow would allow it and stay until way late in October. The majority of the cattle were out and home before he would come down the hill. He would come out as far as Shaver during his time in the mountains, get a supply of groceries and a little bit of whiskey and go back over the hill again. Sam Lee, his son, said that they always raised a garden in what we now call China Camp. They had an irrigation system, mowing machines, and whatever to put up hay for the fall. Sam Lee would ride in as far up to Kaiser until the snow got too deep. This would be like the first part of May. Tie his horse up and walk over the snow and go over to China Camp, plant the garden and stay overnight and then walk back out. He would then get his horse and come back home. Otherwise they did not have a long enough growing season for a lot of his garden to produce, so that was one of the things he did in early Spring…go over early and start the garden. China Camp is southwest of Edison Lake, it is more west, where Mono Creek and the south fork of the San Joaquin River come together, and it is just about two miles due north of that.

Considering how long of a walk it would have been for him, but the guys' work was very physical and most are in pretty good shape. To them it was not that big of a deal.

Charlie was probably an adult when he started staying at China Peak. I know when my parents were first married, in 1922, he was getting quite elderly then and was not going to the mountains any longer, but was still on the ranch. So if he was 65 or 70 at that time, he had to of been born around the mid 1850s or 60s. They brought him to the ranch from San Francisco in 1870 or 1875. He started going to the Rock Meadow country and stuff with the sheep and China Peak that we speak of, probably was a man in his early 20s or maybe even in his teens. He probably started going right away after he got here. But when he started going to China Camp, he had to be a man in his mid 30s.

Laconte was supposed to be a friend of his. He was very knowl-edgeable about everything within his realm, so when Laconte would get in that area, he would always look him up to get any information he could from him. That is why, as a courtesy, he named the mountain after him.

I know there is an old cabin on the backside of China Peak that people attribute to being a cabin that he lived in. Was that true?

I have never gone with him to the cabin. I have been with him a mile from the cabin a million times, but never bothered to go to it. That is when they were running sheep that was the cabin they had. A couple of my great grandfather's sisters came out to California from Alabama. They also got into the livestock business. One of them also had a cabin. Are you familiar with Boneyard Meadow? About a third of the way up from Tamarack there is a meadow called Boneyard. This one descendent came in and settled there. The Perrys and the Greens also had mountain permits. They later switched over to the Woodchuck area.

Some of the places have been Huntington and Shaver Lake. The people still go by it would be interesting to know where you would stop or what Shaver Lake looked like in the early days when you would first go up there.

For myself, Shaver is just like it is today. Prior to that, I know that the stock drive went right through the easterly part of Shaver Lake. The lake is over the top of it now. The building of Shaver Lake as we see it today, some of the medleys say that they got them to build the new trail around the back of Shaver Lake. This is all basically part of the Mono Trail that was originally left over from the Indians and their travel. They keep putting obstacles in the trail in the stories they tell. Lee Blasingame would come up the trail like he always had before and the lake is in the way. Actually it is a channel where Big Creek comes into Huntington. So he looked at the lake and decides that he is not going to change and drives all the cattle out into the lake. It is too far for them to swim and they start drowning. He wasn't too smart, I guess, because they had to abandon that idea.

They have built roads in the way. In fact, kind of a side story, this old guy that worked for my dad when he was a young man. A lot of years had gone by and he got so that he liked the booze pretty good. He asked my dad for a job this one spring going to the mountains. So, for old times sake, my dad gave him a job. Really, the guy was a menace. He always stopped like he was going to adjust his saddle, and he had a bottle of wine hidden in a big coat rolled up on the back of his saddle. As we are coming along Big Creek, where China Peak is now, they were just roughing out the road for the new highway. This old guy is driving the lead bunch of cattle and this dozer is making too much noise, and it is right where the trail is. I asked the guy in the dozer if he would please shut it down for a few minutes while we got through with the cattle. And the guy said he would, but said, "You see that old so-and-so back there? He can't come through here. He is no good." I said that I agreed with him 100% and keep him if you liked. The dozer said that he was his brother-in-law.

My dad ran a slaughter house where the 61 forebay is now, and he furnished the beef for the Edison Company when they were building Florence Lake and building the tunnel through there. They would stay there real late in the fall. This one fall they stayed a little too late and got a big, big storm. They started to come out and the snow was so deep they didn't know if they were going to make it. The Edison Company still had a few packs in there yet, so this one morning these Edison Company guys go by heading over the hill. My dad takes advantage of the situation because they are going to beat the trail out. An hour or two later they finally get packed up and started out of there and they get to the top of Kaiser (right where you come to the sign at the top and start down the south slope), the snow had gotten so deep that a couple of mules had fallen off the trail into the snow on their back. They just rode off and left them, they could not get them out. Anyway, the weather can get a little severe up there.

How many cattle did you slaughter a month?
I can't tell you for sure and I want to say a thousand head, but that seems an awful lot to me. I know that they had livestock scales in there because they bought cattle from the neighbors. All different kinds of people that had mountain permits up there would bring their cattle over and sell them and then would slaughter the cattle. Edison Company had these big coolers. When it got late in the fall, I know my dad would try and fill all these coolers completely full before they left. They slaughtered a few all summer long, but then late in the season they would slaughter twice as many.

Lets start down at Tollhouse. Not much happened on the trail to the mountains until you got to Tollhouse. When the mountain got steep, the troubles got greater. Prior to my time, Tollhouse was all saloons and hotels and stuff and the Teamsters used it when they came off the hill and what have you. They were heavy drinkers, too, most of them. Those days they worked hard and they drank hard. That was the way of life and nobody thought much about it. I know my dad was telling me that when he was a child the road went as far as Shaver and when they come out of the mountains with cattle, they would leave a little spring wagon there at Shaver. This is the chore they always gave the kids or the old men. But he was to drive this spring wagon down and the little mules that they used for pack mules, they hooked to the wagon. They would put all their bedrolls and camp gear and stuff after they unpacked from the pack streams in the wagon. He was coming off the grade and up above what we would call the roadhouse on the old Tollhouse grade, there was lumber wagon tipped over. My dad was 12-years old, but he knew he was as capable as any man, so he decided, well, this wagon had tipped over after the cattle had gone by but before he had come through there, so he decided to unhook the mules from the harness and he is leading his horse behind the wagon also, and puts the pack outfits on the mules. He starts to unload the bedrolls out of the back of the wagon, but they are too heavy and can't lift them up on the mules. After he struggles for about an hour or so, he gets on one of the mules and rides to Tollhouse. All the men had to rent rooms at one of the hotels that night. The next day when he went back to get the bedrolls and things, the Teamsters had already righted the wagon so they helped him put the bedrolls back in the wagon. Children those days did a lot of the work that adults did. When I was like 13-14, the war was on and that is when I started driving. I remember driving up Tollhouse for the first time by myself, kind of the same job that my dad had when he was a kid except we had a pickup instead of a team. We had a real small crew because they were in the war and we started up Tollhouse grade and I helped up to the Roadhouse, then he sent me back to load up this old mare I had in the trailer behind the pickup and load all the bedrolls and stuff in the pickup. I suffered from the same problem my dad did. I got the old mare loaded fine, but when I got to the bedrolls I had a problem with it.

That must have been an adventure driving up and down that grade. I sometimes get a chill when I come around the corner and there is a big motorhome coming towards me and I look over the side and it is pretty steep in a lot of those places. You can imagine what a thirteen-year-old boy looking out, and I was illegally driving anyway, going up that thing. I remember one time, a day or so later when I got up to the Big Creek grade part (it was during the war and you couldn't get any gas, so we carried our gas in these five gallon cans and they always had rust in them anyway), so I poured this gas into that pickup and started up Big Creek and I get up there and it starts plugging up the fuel line. I remember getting out and cleaning out the fuel line. I am not sure if I really knew what I was doing, but I remember my dad had done it. It was sort of a standard thing. Whenever you put gas into the pickup out of a rusty can, you had fuel problems. This older man stopped by and asked if I needed help. I was afraid to tell him I was driving the pickup because I was way too young, so I told him not to worry about it that my dad was out there and would be back in a minute.

The next year the district ranger wanted to make the trip behind Shaver Lake and the new road had not gone in yet. He wanted to make the trip with the cattle up to Huntington, so he drove down there to meet us. At that time Big Creek was the headquarters for the Forest Service. So he said, "I'll tell you what, I need to get my pickup to Huntington." So my dad volunteered my services to drive his pickup to Huntington. Like any normal kid, I was excited about driving someone else's car. After they leave and I get in his pickup and start from Shaver to Huntington, there are all these labels on the dashboard referring to if there was anyone other than an authorized Forest Service personnel driving the vehicle, will be prosecuted. On top of that, I don't even have a valid driver's license and I have to drive up to the town of Big Creek where all the Forest Service people are I about croaked. Couldn't you imagine that happening now? Without a valid driver's license to turn you loose in a government vehicle. Things were pretty slack in those days compared to now.

How did the Australian Shepard become so popular as cattle dogs?

You know, I can't tell you. That was what was available. We had a special breed of dogs. We always had a half female hound and would breed her back with one of these Australian Shepards. The majority of our dogs had about a quarter part hound in them and that gave them better feet and a louder voice and a better nose. They worked very well for the mountains. Since they have come out with other breeds that are a lot more perfected. But our dogs really worked well for us. Down here I use a Border Collie all the time. Which is wonderful for down on the flats, but they are absolutely of no value in the high mountains. They don't bark, and if they find a cow you can't tell where they are. You use the type of dog that works well for the type of country you are in.

My dad's uncle was Bud Sample and his permit was up Kings River just up on the bench above Tehipite. When my dad was a kid he would go up there, past Crown Valley and on up that way, with Bud. And Bud always had these hounds, or at least a hound or two, and he loved to run the bears. The bears were extremely thick in that area. Dad's chore every morning after breakfast he would get up, and they would kill this bear. They had this old bear hide and he would get on his horse and they would drag the bear hide around the hillside and different places and tie it up in a tree someplace after he made this mile or so run. Then after they would break camp, Bud would turn the hound pups loose and they would track that bear down. They were training their bear dogs. Bud's favorite deal was to rope them. In fact, everybody tried to rope them. They were packing supplies in from Shaver to Huntington Lake and my dad was coming out, and just about where China Peak is, they were coming out and an Indian boy jumped this yearling bear. So they decided they would have a good time and try to rope it. They had come to this tamarack tree and it climbs the tree, but right along side of it there was another tamarack tree, so they decided that they could not rope the bear if it was in the tree. So my dad proceeded to get everything all fixed up and said that he was going to climb the tree and when this thing comes down, you rope it. So my dad climbs this tree parallel to the bear and he has this big limb that he is poking at the bear. The bear runs down the tree part way and my dad starts down the tree but steps on a dead limb and falls to the ground...and beats the bear to the ground. The bear climbs back up the tree, but my dad is kind of shook up so he tells the Indian boy to climb the tree. So the Indian boy climbed the tree and got the bear to come back down and proceeded to rope the bear. They decided to put the bear on the packhorse and take it out. They had its legs tied up, but they put this stick out and the bear snaps the stick. They then put a noose over its nose so it would not bite. It was a long ways on horseback from China Peak to Shaver and in the process this rope they tied around the nose got too tight and it smothered the bear. They get to Shaver and unpack it and find that the bear is dead. They were wondering what they would do with a dead bear when this guy comes by that he went to high school with that had a motorcycle. The guy asked what they were going to do with that dead bear. The guy takes the bear and there was a newspaper write-up about how this guy on a motorcycle had captured a bear. This was probably before 1920.

What were they going to do with a live bear?
I don't know, but I had cages full of bobcats and coyotes and foxes and stuff as a kid. I always thought you were supposed to have those kinds of things.
We lived in Fresno when I was a kid, too, and we had these things in our backyard. We lived right there where Fresno High School is located. We had cages full of hawks and stuff.

Tell the story about the two men killed up near Graveyard Meadows and how Graveyard Meadows got its name.
This is just hearsay as I did not experience it myself. It had to have been in the early 1900s and these were apparently the French Basque who were running sheep in there. That had been a sheep range for William Temple Cole and apparently he got too old and everyone was in there trying to grab this feed.
These Basque were using some range the Cole family had used prior to the Basque coming in. There had been some arguing back and forth for a period of time, and apparently the Basque were

having breakfast and they had their plates and cups and sitting on a log and were ambushed by the Coles. I am not sure how many were killed, I know it was more than two, and it seems to me there were like three or four. Someone buried them in a shallow grave there and later on that year they came back and got Charlie Lee, the Chinaman, to go back and dig them up and put them in a sack. They gave Charlie something like five or ten bucks and a fifth of whiskey to go to that chore. They moved the bodies and reburied them. I do know that the meadow that they call Graveyard Meadow is actually a good two miles above the site where those people were actually ambushed. When I was young there used to be some Aspen trees in there that had big Xs carved on them. If you were coming out of Edison Lake on the trail that goes to Goodale Pass, the site was probably two to two and a half miles up from Edison Lake. The meadow that they call Graveyard is what the old-timers all called Cole Canyon, after this William Temple Cole who had been in there real early with sheep.

What were some of the things that went on with the sheep ranchers and the cattle ranchers in the early days of the Huntington area?

You know in the movies they always show the sheep men and the cattlemen always fighting each other. This was not the problem in our area because all of them had been in the sheep business prior to the Forest Service becoming active. After the Forest Service became a major part in it, then they converted from sheep to cattle. So you didn't have the cattleman and sheep man fighting as you did the original forty-niners who had turned into sheep producers between those and the later coming as the French Basque because they had established what they thought was their territory, or their permits, and didn't have any legal right to them. Later on, in comes in the French Basque who said that the others didn't have any right to it any more than the French Basque did, and they were going to use the land.

Up at Blaney Meadow, John Ship was the man with the sheep permit there, and he actually had a deed to some of the ground there at Blaney. The Basque came in and started using some of what he considered his feed and his range. They had a little squabble back and forth, and the Basque said that he could not keep them out. He said that one thing he could do was to say that that was his bridge and his property, and the first guy that walks across that bridge I will shoot. In the process, he shot two and killed them. Then he went down and turned himself in to the authorities. They had a hearing and a trial on it, and I don't think he got reprimanded on it very seriously.

There was another happening of this kind. It was an uncle to my dad. Lee Blasingame was his name. This was before the Forest Service became active. They would winter over on the west side and come back in the summer to the Sierras. Lee got into an argument with another one of the families in the area. This Corlew decided Lee was feeding off of some of the ground that was his and so to retaliate he went over and shot about a dozen or so of Lee's ewes. Lee became upset, and he was not the kind of guy that had a mild temperament, but was noted to be too stringent at times. Lee goes to look up Corlew, who, at that time, was staying in a cabin about two miles down the new grade from where the school-house is at Pine Ridge. There are some little apple orchards in that area. So Lee goes up and bangs on the door and calls Corlew out, and they get into a fight. Lee beats the devil out of Corlew. When Lee finally leaves, Corlew is on the floor semiconscious, or maybe completely unconscious, I don't know. Lee goes out and gets on his horse and starts to ride off. In the meantime, Corlew came to and managed to get his shotgun out from behind the door and called out to Lee. As Lee turned around to look at him, the first shot caught him in the mouth and blew all his teeth out and the next shot hit the horse in the butt and threw Lee off and kicked Lee, causing him to have a broken arm and leg. And with that, Corlew went back inside the cabin and closed the door. After Lee became conscious, he crawled from there clear down to where Sierra High School is currently to the Medley's who kept him alive until his mother was able to come and drive him down to Fresno to a doctor.

I know they tell the story about her being a widow lady at that time and she hooked her horse up to the buggy (they lived right down where the old Frontier Chevrolet was in downtown Fresno...they called it the Blasingame block at one time) and they say she almost ran it to death getting up to get to where Lee was.

This Lee was also a character. Another thing he did, the Forest Service came along and told him he could no longer take his sheep to the mountains. But he also had quite a bunch of horses. He had an old guy by the name of Beau Sealy who was some kind of an uncle or cousin to him, that was tending the sheep at the time, and they were running up the side of the grade, underneath the schoolhouse there at Cressman's on that hillside, he had two bands of sheep there. The Forest Service knew what he was thinking about doing and had a guy watching him every day. He had binoculars and watched that he would not sneak into the mountains. The year before they had told him he could not go to the mountains and he went anyway. He goes to see this Beau Sealy and tells him that tonight when the Forest Service guy goes home, you split that band of sheep in half and take it into the mountains and split the remaining in half and when the Forest Service guy comes back in the morning he will still see two bands of sheep. The funny part is, they had to drive the sheep about fifty yards from the ranger station to get into the mountains and they slipped by there during the night real quiet-like. The next morning he runs his band of loose horses by there to take out the tracks from the sheep so that the Forest Service guys could not catch him. This type of activity was done a lot in those days.

Another question for you, and this has to do with equipment and things people used in the mountains in the old days opposed to what they use today.

Things were pretty primitive in those days. Everybody had a slicker, a saddle slicker, which was an oilskin slicker that when you were on horseback it covered you completely down to your feet. That was a standard part of your gear. You also had a felt hat that usually leaked like hell after it rained a little bit. The first thing you did was knocked the crown out so there was no crease in it so the rain would run off better. You stayed wet and cold all the time. Your boots, well, they were always leaking. I remember one summer being back there myself, and being the young man that I was, I just had my boots I was wearing and did not take any extra

106

shoes. It rained everyday that summer and my feet stayed wet all the time. I could not get my boots on and off, so finally I put a little bit of grease on the inside of my instep so that I could get my foot in the boots. To get the water out of them, I cut them just above where they were fastened to the sole. They actually were not much of boot by the time you got done.

Another thing that they wore, and this was more of a fashion, but usable thing, and this was they wore these mohair chaps. They were just a thing that was in style in the early 1900s. My dad had a pair of them what were white with spots that were dyed purple. So he was dapper. Then they went into the phase where they wore these things called jodhpurs, the blooming pants, and they had these lace up boots that came up to the knees. The cowboys did not wear them, but I had an uncle that did and a couple of aunts that wore these things. But that certainly was not standard cowboy procedure. In those days, when you bought a pair of Levis you bought the waist size. They all came extremely long, like thirty-six inches or longer, so if you had a thirty-inch inseam, you just rolled the cuffs up. Every old cowboy as I was growing up had these big high rolled cuffs. Everybody had a bull-derm string sticking out of their pocket, these pants rolled up like that, and usually a felt hat that was mostly worn out. When I was young no one had straw hats. They wore felt hats summer and winter.

One set of clothes for summer and one for winter?
You had the pair you had on and you usually rolled another set in your bedroll. A lot of time we were away from the cabin. Like when we would be in Devil's Den or up by Silver Pass and that country, or over to Lake Ione or off in the Fish Creek country, sometimes we would be gone ten days. Also, we had a major camp up at Big Meadow, which is in the bottom of Edison Lake now, just behind where that little store is. That was our summer camp and you would camp out on the ground all summer.

What about bathing? What did you do for that all summer?
It was very limited. At the main camp you probably had a big old washtub. They are the long oval ones. If you got to where you could not really stand it, you would heat up some water on the fire

and take a bath. Otherwise you would jump in the creek once in a while and wash the best that you could. Every couple of days you had to do some of your own laundry because you didn't carry that much with you. The clothes you took with you amounted to one change, but you would have another set at China Camp at the cabin. When you left camp, you had the one set you wore and another set rolled up in you bed. In your bed was your house, where you had a double length canvas that your sleeping bag went in. Another thing that was a very important part of your gear and you hesitated taking it because they were so heavy, but it was a Dutch oven. After you are in the mountains for three to four days, you have eaten up all the bread that you brought from town. The bread that you got after that was usually biscuits or cornbread and you made that in the Dutch oven. The Dutch oven became a very universal tool. You could fry in it, make stew, bake in it, so you took it with you even though it was extremely heavy and you tried to keep your packs as light as possible. In fact, today the kids ask me to cook in the Dutch oven for them. And we usually do make a trip every summer where I do a little bit of that.

They have a big Dutch oven cook-off in Shaver Lake in the summer now with the Historical Society.
Before that evolved to Shaver, they had that at Huntington for a few years at a friend's cabin. They asked me to come up one year and to cook something in a Dutch oven, so I go up there and doing what I have been doing all my life. We used to dig a hole about the depth of the Dutch oven and a little bit bigger and we would build a fire in that hole and when it burned down to coals you would take a shovel and take out about ninety five percent of the coals and put on the lid and set the Dutch oven in the hole. All the earth all around it was already heated up and it was a better insulated thing. When I went up to Huntington, he had this big steel surface and all these briquettes that they have. The first thing you did when you bought a Dutch oven is saw the legs off of it because those legs would put holes in the kayaks while you were packing. All these guys had these Dutch ovens on legs and they would set these charcoal briquettes. They had it down to such a science; they knew just how many briquettes to cook a certain meal. So here I am,

kind of backwoods, and I get out there and used some dead limbs and made a fire and made some biscuits and some other things. None of the rest uses that style of cooking. There is a guy in Clovis called Cookie that gives lessons on Dutch oven baking and some of these guys had taken lessons from him. These guys have made some unbelievable things that they cooked, where we were just down to basics; the biscuits, the cornbread, and would do a roast occasionally, lots of stews, and had even been used as a dishpan in a pinch. Although with some of the Dutch oven guys if you touched it with soap they had a fit.

Would you tell a little bit of how you used to keep meat and how you would store your food up there without any refrigeration?
We did eat fresh meat sometimes. You could only take enough meat up from the Valley to last four or five days and then you were without meat for the rest of the year unless you had enough ingenuity to figure out something else to eat. We had white sacks that we put over the carcasses in the daytime and would hang them in the tree so they had ventilation all the time. We would not lay them down because the meat would sweat. In the daytime, you hung them up in the shade with this cover on them. At night as soon as the sun went down and the flies went away, then you pulled the cover off and let it completely air out at night and you could keep meat a surprisingly long time. In the fall, it would last for ten days to two weeks. When I say fall time, I mean it is after it gets good and cold.

Any competition from mountain lions or other animals?
The bear were a nuisance. In 1941 we build a cabin at China Camp, and the bears were so bad. See, the Forest Service and the Park Service came into a practice, and they spoiled the bears so bad over at Yosemite or at one of the parks, they would trap it and bring it over here to turn it loose. They didn't break the bear's habits at all; they just moved him to new territory. Any cabin they came to they would ravish it, and their favorite thing was to tear down the door going in, tear up everything and put holes in canned goods and usually eave their calling card on the table or some-

place. They did not think much of you; they wanted to show you what they thought. Then they would go out through the roof on the way out. They didn't just destroy a little bit, they ruined everything. So in 1941 they build this cabin, I was just a kid at the time but was involved in it, and they did not put any windows in it and the ceiling had solid logs also and the door had a real heavy steel cover on it. That did keep the bears out. It was our bear-proof cabin. Anything that the bear could destroy as soon as we left camp we put in that cabin, otherwise when we got back it was always ruined. But prior to that cabin and even after the cabin was built, we would close the door but we never locked the door. When anyone came by and needed something to eat, they were welcome to whatever was there. It was an unwritten law that whatever you used, the next time you came by you replenished it. And this worked great until the early 1950s when the people of the mountains totally changed. All of a sudden everybody had a surplus jeep and a GI rifle and the mountains became totally alive with people. Prior to that, you were either related or knew one another very well.

What can you remember back of the early recreational use that was going on in the mountains?
There you had different levels. All the foothillers, when I say all I mean a big majority, migrated to the higher elevations during the summertime because it was so hot down here. Like the Ockendens, they had a ranch at Academy and they summered up there by Shaver at Ockenden. The Musicks that you know, one of the fields we had was called Musicks Flats. The Blasingames, the Samples, and the Simpsons all had places in the mountains. So when it got good and hot down here, they were up there with livestock anyway, so they got up there where it was cooler. Then, of course the Edison Company, first it was logging deals then it evolved to the Edison Company and their power projects. So then it began to fill up with other people from Fresno and what have you to summer vacation.
It is kind of funny how the animals and stuff has changed. Prior to World War II, there was deer in the mountains, but no large abundance to them. If you were a good hunter you could get a deer and

110

I think it was a two-deer season in those days. Then World War II came and all the men went to war so, by the time those five years of the war was going on and a year or so to recuperate after the war, there had not been anyone shooting deer in like six or seven years. So the population had just become enormous and at that time all the boys out of the foothills had gone because prior to that, a deer never survived a week in the foothills because if one had gotten down that far a foothiller had ate it.

There for fifteen years, the deer population in the foothills was just unbelievable. I can remember seeing herds of deer. You spoke of running into a deer with a car one time, well, in that area I could remember running into a herd of deer that had at least fifty or more in a bunch. After the war it did not take long for that surplus to disappear. We are down now to where in the high Sierras there are not enough deer to count. There are a few left in the foothills just because the landowners protect them. But the Forest Service itself, the deer population is just nil. The mountain lions have also gotten them. You cannot take away the predator of the lion.

During prohibition and those times up in the mountains, do you have any stories about stills or people running whiskey up in the mountains?

There is one story that I remember. My dad, about that time was running a slaughterhouse and killing beef for the Edison Company when they were building Florence Lake and putting the tunnel in to Huntington. There was a single lady called "Six-Shooter Kate" and she lived over there, will be about mid to two-thirds up Pine Flat Reservoir, and she lived on the south side of that. Through the prohibition times she would take these pack horses full of booze and go into the mountains and sell at the logging camps and then go over to sell to the Edison camp employees. This one time she was camped over at 61 selling this bootleg whiskey. My dad said she dug a hole when she first came into camp and buried all of her whiskey, then covered it up with dirt and built a fire on top of it so when the authorities came to search her out she did not have any whiskey. This one time they got kind of wise to her and figured her out and they did this raid one night and caught her red-handed. They took her off to jail. Someone hauled her horses off and took care of those for her. The old blue dog she had no one paid any attention to it, so it got left there. Eventually the dog came over to my dad's camp at the slaughterhouse and stayed with him. Six-Shooter Kate was in jail for a long period of time, so my dad just kept the dog. The next year, coming out of the mountains we would put our cattle in what we called the Letcher Place, which is fork where Sample Road and Tollhouse Road come together. We would always corner the cattle in Letcher and it would take two or three days every fall to separate the dry cows from the cows and calves and this type of thing. This one time my dad is out there and this car stops out on the highway and this old woman jumps out and whistles and yells, "Come, Blue." My dad said that was the last time he ever saw that dog. It acted like he never even knew my dad. He jumped in that car with her, she slammed the door and away they went. Other than that, as far as bootleggers and stills in that country, I don't know any more stories on it. Most of the stories I am telling you are not written history because I was fortunate in being raised in a nitch in time and was raised with these old guys who had done this all their life. A lot of them were getting quite elderly when I was growing up, and I just ate it all up. Every night after dinner, whether we were sitting around the campfire when we were camped out or over at one of the cabins, they would start telling these stories. I did live in an unusual situation where we lived in town all the school year, then the second school was out we were in the mountains until school started again in the fall. So I sort of lived a combination of both lives. The trades and stuff I was learning as a kid was something that was already passé, it was over. So by the time I learned it quite well there was no need for it, but I did like it and it was a great part of my life.

One last story.

Run back off the grade and nylon ropes were brand new then. They had just come out, and I saved enough money together to get a new nylon rope. Well, this cow runs back and the dogs were on her, and I could not turn her. She thinks her calf has gone back and is going to go look for it. The first time I got any open ground was about the time I was in front of the store heading down the road, so

I roped this cow. When you are by yourself like that, if you kind of give the cows a real bad jar, they will turn around and go back to the bunch quite often. So I roped the cow and, what we call tripping, I rode on by the cow, and what you do is throw the rope behind the rump and then put on your turns and ride by and this will flip the cow right around in the air and throw her on her side. It was a little rough, but was a procedure that we used all the time. This particular time the cow fell on top of my new nylon rope and that pavement just ruined this rope. I remember getting up and was really upset about losing my rope. Pulled the rope off the cow and she started back up the road to the bunch, and Mrs. Yancey is pointing her finger at me for being mean to the cow.

Carrie & Chris at Rancheria Falls,
Huntington Lake

HIKE NUMBER 15
Rancheria Falls

Category: Easy
Length: 2 Miles Round Trip
Time: 60-90 Minutes
Maps: U.S.G.S. Kaiser Peak and Huntington Lake Quadrangles

Directions From Shaver Lake
From the hardware store in the middle of the village of Shaver Lake, drive northeast on Route 168. Pass the Sierra Summit Ski area and turn right at 19.5 miles. This side road is marked Rd 8S31. Sometimes there is even a sign for Rancheria Falls. Travel up this predominantly logging road 1.25 miles to the trailhead for Rancheria Falls.

Parking
There is generally ample parking at the trailhead.

General Description
This is one of the best-known and easiest walks in the Huntington Lake region. This trail is unique because it has been constructed to be wheelchair accessible. The trail is also very popular with families and is, for many, a traditional Spring outing.

The Route
The trail ascends very gradually from the parking area and continues its benign meander approximately 1.0 mile to the entrance of the Rancheria Falls area. Here, the trail turns sharply right and enters the small valley of the falls. The route is obvious and does not require any special direction.

From the entrance to the fall's valley, the trail proceeds to the base of the falls, but your final stop will depend on the season of the year and the spirit of the group. In early spring, the falls provide one of the best natural shows in the area. The spray and mist will cool you instantly, and again, depending on the time of the year,

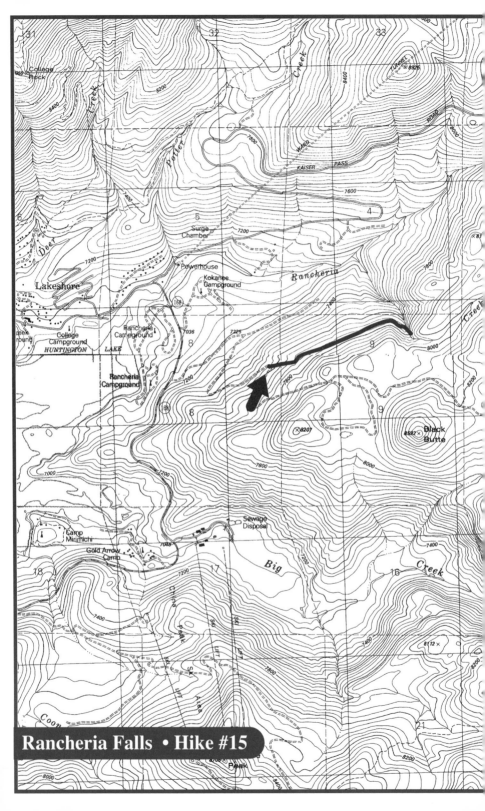

Rancheria Falls • Hike #15

you will be able to gauge your own final destination.

Cautions
The trail to the fall's valley is fairly flat and safe. However, the last part of the trail into the falls' valley is along a steep hillside. This can be dangerous in the early spring when late snowfields make for slippery going. This section of the trail can also give the less than intrepid a goose bump or two. With small children, I would recommend a line (rope) of some kind. For your peace of mind, don't volunteer to guide your sister-in-law's attention deficit/ hyperactivity disordered son on this hike. If you do, you will wish you had taken a little something for your nerves by the time you get back!

Special Attractions
Needless to say, it's those falls. There are some attractive wild-flowers on the trail, and returning you will get some tantalizing peeks at Huntington Lake. But this trip really features the water-fall. If a little privacy is what you are after, when you come out of the falls valley, turn sharply left and climb straight up the hill to the top of the falls. You will be one in a million in visitor status, and only the marmots will be there to greet you. The peace and seren-ity there is truly worth the work.

*Doug & Chloe, trail crew on Ely Mountain,
Shaver Lake*

HIKE NUMBER 16
Black Butte

Category: Moderate
Length: 1 Mile Round Trip
Time: 90 Minutes
Map: U.S.G.S. Huntington Lake Quadrangle

Directions From Shaver Lake

From the hardware store in the center of the village of Shaver Lake, drive northeast on Route 168. Drive past the Sierra Summit Ski Area and turn right at the sign indicating Huntington Lake Recreation Area (19.7 miles). This road is also designated Road 8S31. Follow this road past the trailhead for Rancheria Falls (20.4 miles). Continue until you have traveled 22.6 miles. Look for an area of new growth lodgepole pine on the left. Directly across from the new growth, that is, on the right side of the road, seek a small cairn marking the start of the trail.

Parking

Parking is available along the right side of the road. There is ample room for other vehicles to pass your parked car.

General Description

Black Butte rewards the hiker with the best of all views of Huntington Lake. From Black Butte's summit, the entire lake is visible. As you look down the length of the lake, you will always remember the summit on which you stand.
Black Butte also provides a great vantagepoint for viewing Red Mountain, China Peak (Sierra Summit), and Mount Givens. For the intrepid, this little peak is a full adventure!

The Route

Following the cairns from the roadside, head up the hillside. Using your sharp eye, you will see the cairns laid out ahead generally leading in a southeasterly direction. Switching left and then right,

119

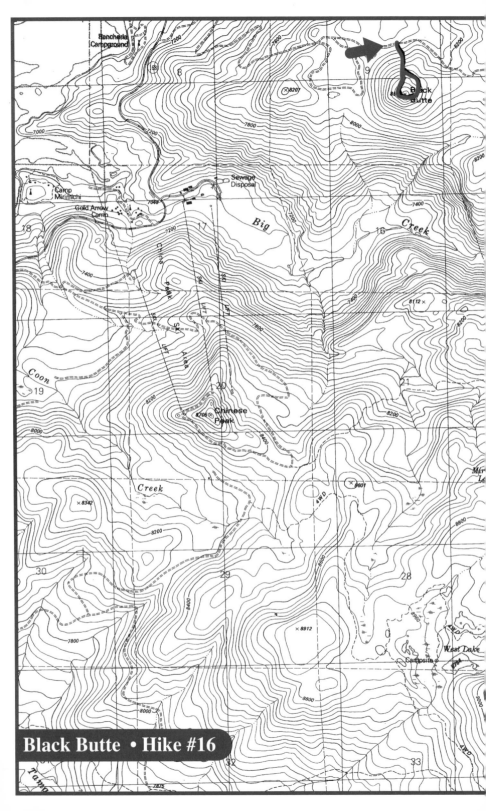

Black Butte • Hike #16

the vague trail brings the hiker to the base of a large boulder field. Boulders comprise the greater part of the scramble to the summit. To assist the hiker, a series of cairns have been set to guide you to the top. Though not necessary to the completion of this rock piles ascension, the cairns indicate a fairly straightforward track.

As the boulder field is entered, a large red fir stands as a sentry. Climbing past this landmark, follow the cairns up the large plates of granite that make your path. Further along, there is a clearing between two stands of red fir. Make your way between them, favoring the right side of the clearing.

The path traverses right between some mountain laurel. This group of laurel carpets the base of the summit cone. Here you will get the first of the views of the lake. Take your best guess and scramble up the remaining few feet of the climb.

Arriving on the summit (8,598 feet), you will have hiked a scant half-mile, but it certainly won't feel like that!

Cautions

This short scramble is full of loose rock. There are many opportunities to lose one's balance or turn an ankle. This is not a good choice for the faint of heart, inexperienced hikers, or pets other than goats! As mass wasting (the geologic phenomenon whereby gravity exerts its influence to bring all things to equilibrium, like the valley floor) exerts its mighty influence, be careful not to have one of those large boulders come crashing down on any part of you!

Special Attractions

The view and the challenge to see it are the ingredients that make this trek one of the best in the region. You will always remember your visit to the top as you observe Black Butte's rocky peak from Sierra Summit or any of the other beautiful spots around Huntington Lake.

Vernal Pools on the last section of Table Mountaiin

HIKE NUMBER 17
Big Creek and Indian Pools

Category: Easy
Length: 4 Miles Round Trip
Time: 2 Hours
Map: U.S.G.S. Huntington Lake Quadrangle

Directions From Shaver Lake
From the hardware store in the center of the village of Shaver Lake, head northeast on Highway 168. Follow this road 18.4 miles to the entrance to Sierra Summit Ski Area.

Parking
Parking is readily available in the large parking lot directly across from the entrance to the ski area.

General Description
The trail along Big Creek is easily negotiated and very pleasant for a family outing. This hike is also perfect for combinations of interests such as birding, picnicking, fishing, and a swim in the refreshing waters. Loaded with vast varieties of wildflowers in mid-season, the hike to Indian Pools and beyond has much to recommend it!

The Route
Beginning at the entrance to the ski area, follow the access road to the end of the last parking lot. Keeping the creek to your right, enter the woods at a point just beyond the first of the staff trailers (.45 miles). Near the creek's edge, you will immediately find the trail.

The trail is quite flat in the beginning, and it may be muddy in early spring conditions. It soon begins to gradually ascend along the creek's edge, giving beautiful views of the cascades below you. At your feet, you will observe a low ground cover of arctostapholos, uva-ursi.

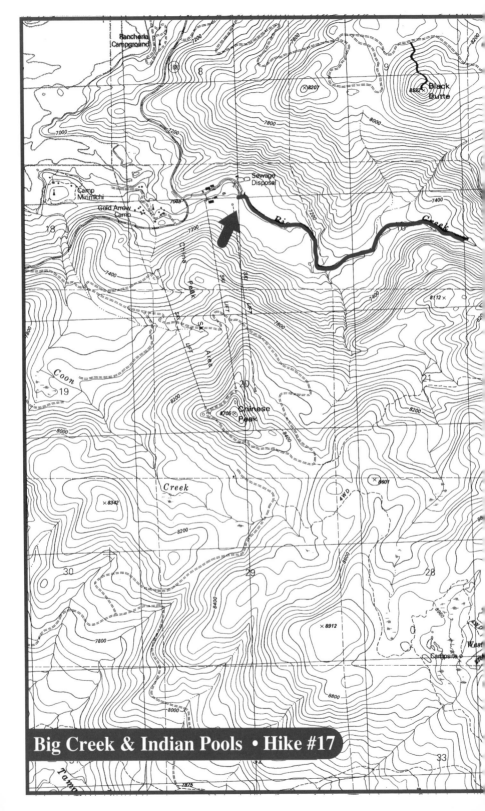

Big Creek & Indian Pools • Hike #17

This dwarf manzanita yields a white, snowberry in the fall. In a short distance (1.06 miles) you will reach Indian Pools. The pools are a great place for a picnic or even as a destination. Mind the "No Camping" sign in the area. Overuse of the Indian Pool's area has caused its closing as a campsite. Those desirous of a campsite will find ample spots a short distance up the trail.

The trail continues toward the left generally following the course of Big Creek. Although vague at times, the trail is consistent in its mission leading you upstream. At 1.5 miles, the trail turns and descends toward a small pond in the creek. From here, head left into a small aspen grove. In another .1 mile you will ascend a rocky plateau and continue into a meadow rich with Mule Ear flowers in mid to late June.

Walking along, you soon reach a small waterfall (1.8 miles). This is the first of a series of falls that lead to the walk's culmination at a large, swimable pool (2.1 miles). To make this even more appealing, there is a lovely falls filling the pool and a cluster of mountain ash growing from the rocky cliff on the opposite shore. The trail does continue from this point, however, negotiating the trail becomes increasingly hazardous. Because this is not a maintained route, it is recommended only for experienced hikers and mountaineers.

Cautions

Because this trail is not maintained, following the route can be a bit tricky. Remembering that the route follows the creek will keep you on track. In early spring, the waters are swift and eschewing the shore is advisable.

Special Attractions

Wildflowers, fishing, and ease of access make this one of the premier day walks in the Huntington area. Skiers can also take joy in views of some of the more challenging runs on the Sierra Summit face. In the fall, when the aspen are golden colored, that is the time to "Think Snow"!

Susan at Balsam Forebay, Huntington Lake

HIKE NUMBER 18
Camp 72 Road

Category: Moderate
Length: 7 Miles Round Trip
Time: 3.5 Hours
Map: U.S.G.S. Huntington Lake Quadrangle

Directions from Shaver Lake
From the hardware store in the middle of downtown Shaver Lake, drive north approximately 8.7 miles on Route 168. The start of the walk is just past the snow park at Balsam Forebay.

Parking
Immediately past the snow park entrance on the left, is the access road and path of the Camp 72 trail. Parking is ample at the trailhead.

General Description
On a cool and crisp autumn morning, Charles Fergusson, Pam Geisel, and I made the trek in search of Camp 72. Camp 72 was the base of operations for the tunnel drillers boring the tunnel's path from Huntington Lake to Shaver. The camp was located approximately half way between the two lakes, and it made the perfect location for an adit. An adit is an entrance to a tunnel, generally half way along its course, designed to ease the removal of tunnel tailings from the drilling process.
The adit is closed by a steel door, but the site of the tailings clearly reveals itself to the walker. We never found the camp's location. After a long search, we returned to the adit and enjoyed our lunch!

The Route
The trail (road) begins at highway 168 and soon (0.2 miles) opens to some nice views of the Chiquinto Range. Continuing, the road crosses a small brook by a washed out culvert (0.7 miles). As the road snakes left and right, you will pass a variety of vegetation:

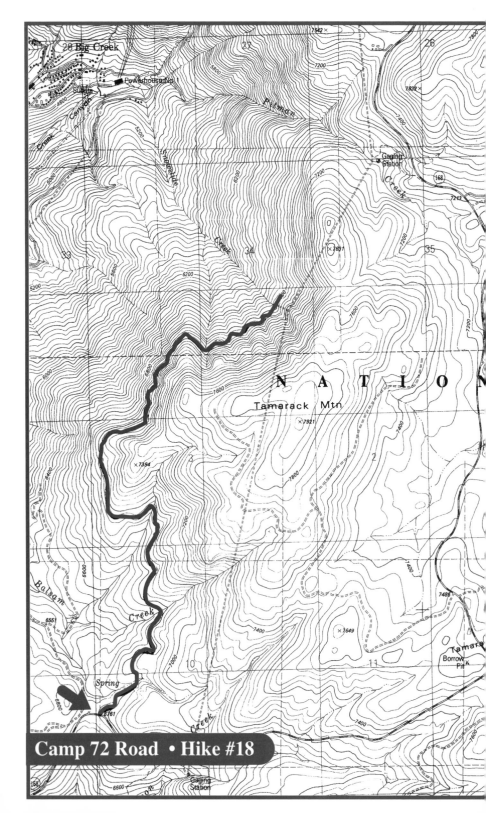

Camp 72 Road • Hike #18

alder, willow, winterberry, forget-me-not, and penstemon.

At 1.3 miles, you will cross another stream and in a short distance, you will round the canyon's end (1.4 miles). This spot is marked by a spring and from the characteristics of the land, it may have been a watering hole for horses.

Past the spring, an interesting group of boulders surrounds the road. These appear to be glacial erratics, large boulders deposited by the last glacier. Soon views begin to appear. Vistas of Big Creek and the surrounding hills are exciting to behold. At 2.4 miles, you will pass a group of ledges that may make a good spot for bouldering. A mile farther, you will reach the adit!

Cautions

This road is open to vehicle traffic during certain times of the year.

Special Attractions

This is a nice long walk. It is interesting to think of the miners living on the side of the mountain and carving the tunnel. This was very dangerous work, and the conditions the miners experienced were severe.

Susan & Gregory at Balsam Forebay, Huntington Lake

HIKE NUMBER 19
Balsam Forebay

Category: Easy
Length: 2.5 Miles Round Trip
Time: 90 Minutes
Maps: U.S.G.S. Huntington Lake and Musick Mountain Quadrangles

Directions From Shaver Lake

From the hardware store in the center of the village of Shaver Lake, drive approximately 8.7 miles north on Route 168 toward Huntington Lake. Stop at the first snow park on your left.

Parking

There is, generally, ample and safe parking in the large lot designed for the snow park use. There is also a toilet facility for the nasally insensitive! I prefer natural pine scent.

There is a requirement for a parking permit to use the snow park between the months of November and Memorial Day. The permits may be obtained at the Shaver Lake hardware store or from your local ranger station. Unfortunately, those lacking the permit are fined $75.00! If you are without a permit as you read this description and your car is in the aforementioned lot, park across Route 168 from the snowpark.

General Description

This walk features splendid views of Kaiser Ridge behind the foreground of this lovely, man-made lake. The entire area has been designated by the Southern California Edison Company as a wildlife enhancement area. One spring day, while cross-country skiing around the forebay, I saw ten or more coyotes on the far shore gathering duck eggs for their morning repast. During the summer and fall, I have seen many signs of deer activity.

131

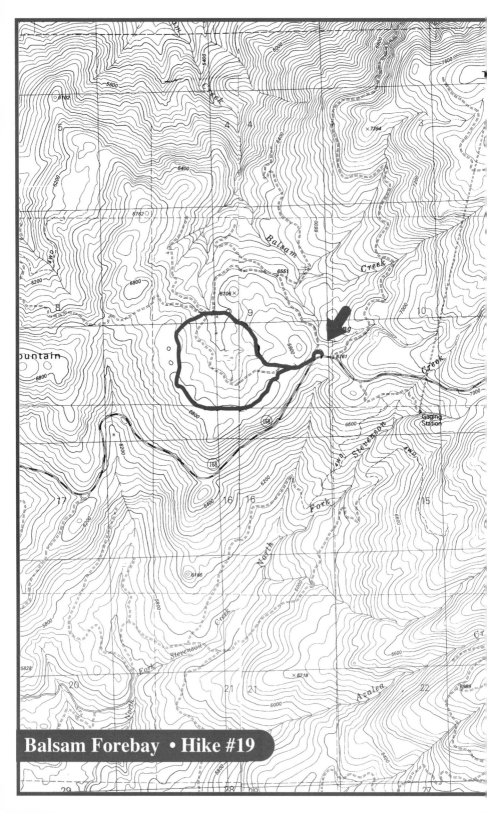

Balsam Forebay • Hike #19

The Route

Beginning on a road just behind the "Outhouse," head up the hill approximately .2 miles to a sign indicating a picnic area to the right. Continue left past the sign until you reach a powerhouse (.66 miles). In low water, you can go down to the shore and follow along the sand to the dam. I prefer to follow the road just behind the powerhouse up and above the quarry overlooking the lake. From the top of the hill, follow the road west and then turn north at the first power pole. The trail becomes a bit obscure as you wend your way east back to the forebay.

Turn right onto the spillway and proceed due east toward the dam (1.4 miles). Walk across the top of the dam to the far side. There you will continue right on a road connecting you to the picnic area. The picnic area has a plaque honoring the Mono Indians that first inhabited this area. On one of the rocks in the rest area, a skillful eye will detect an Indian grinding hole. From the picnic area (also outhouse equipped), it is an easy walk back to the car to complete this 2.5 mile loop.

(Since I wrote this description, a new trail has been added to this loop. The new trail leaves from the parking lot and heads west to meet the woods road that circles the forebay. If you choose to use this as the access to the trail circling the forebay, it works just as well as the above-mentioned track.)

Cautions

Be cautious with small children when crossing the dam. The west side is steep and unprotected. Otherwise this is a safe and pleasant hike.

Special Attractions

The fact the this area is protected for wildlife makes it attractive for anyone interested in birding, wild flowers, or other natural attractions. The coyotes and deer seem to abound here. When the forebay is full, it is especially attractive. One day during the Big Creek fire in 1996, I witnessed several large helicopters dipping into the lake to pick up water with which they were fighting the fire. It was a very exciting show!

Greg & Andy on a springtime neighborhood walk,
Shaver Lake

HIKE NUMBER 20
The S. J. & E. Railroad Grade
Shaver Crossing to Dawn

Category: Easy/Moderate
Length: Variable from 1-56 Miles Round Trip
Time: 1 Hour and Up
Map: U.S.G.S. Musick Mountain Quadrangle

Directions From Shaver Lake
From the hardware store drive approximately 4.25 miles east to the Huntington Lake Road. Turn left toward the town of Big Creek. At 7.1 miles from the hardware store, you will encounter the trailhead on your left. This area is clearly marked with a sign indicating the S. J. & E. Railroad Grade.

Parking
Parking is available immediately off the road in the area adjacent to the sign marking the railroad's former presence.

General Description
The S. J. & E grade is historically significant as well as aesthetically appealing. A walk that can be easily adapted to any schedule or group inclination (mountain biking, jogging, or walking), the S. J. & E. grade can offer beautiful views of the San Joaquin river basin, the Yosemite National Park, and the southern slopes of Kaiser Peak. Built in 1912 in a period of just 157 days, this nostalgic route through the mountains features wildflowers, waterfalls, and dogwood blossoms in the spring. This walk also contains structures of the local economic and industrial history of the evolution of the Edison Company's presence in Shaver Lake. Of more modern significance along the route, a walker can observe the penstocks and powerhouses that produce our electricity today. For a further description of the route, the video, The Story of the SJ & E, can bring the past to life. This film by the Central Sierra Historical Society is a fun way to psyc up your hiking cronies or to make educational a wonderful day in the mountains.

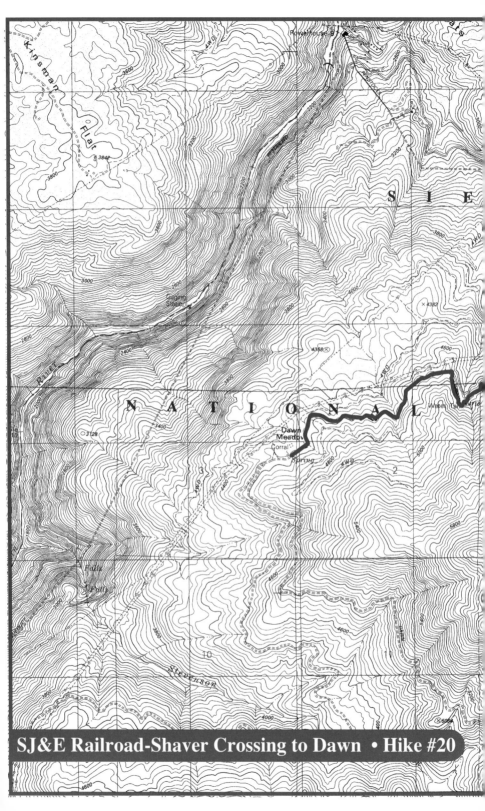

SJ&E Railroad-Shaver Crossing to Dawn • Hike #20

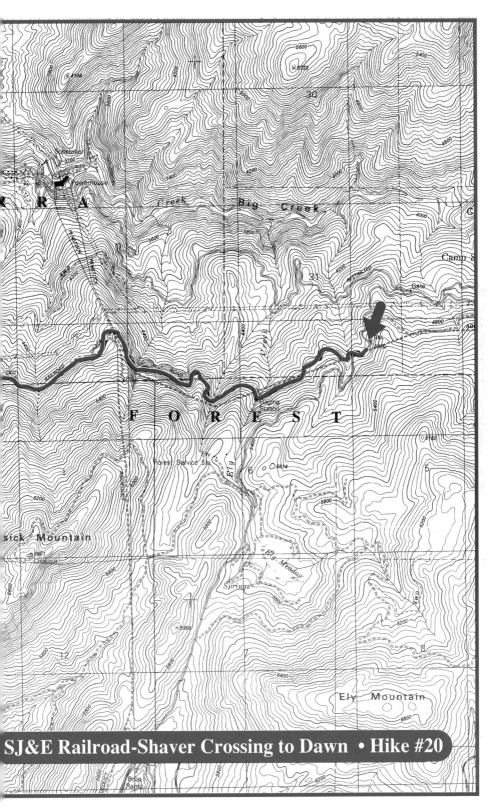

SJ&E Railroad-Shaver Crossing to Dawn • Hike #20

The Route

From the parking lot on the Huntington Lake Road, walk 0.2 miles to the charming and rustic cabin that marks the top of the climb that began in the valley. Continue along to a penstock (pipe) at .7 miles that identifies Ely Creek. This watercourse cascades down to Southern California Edison Company's PowerHouse 2.

From the Ely Creek water station, the road snakes its way along the north side of Musick Mountain. This part of the road has fantastic views of the Clark Range and the back of Yosemite National Park. The road continues to the main penstock (just past MP 21, a brown post meaning "Mile Post"). This pipe is used to transport water from Shaver Lake to PowerHouse Number 2. The penstock was specially designed and built in Germany and moved to its present location by the railroad. Of interest here are the vent pipes that stand prominently on the horizon. Without these vents, the force of the suction from the cascading water inside the pipe would cause the steel to collapse!

Just beyond the penstock on the left, the curious will find an abandoned rail car and track. Imagining the men working through the summer rushing to complete this project can bring the scene to life!

The road continues to a series of two bridges built to skirt the steep cliffs (1.8 miles) on the back of the mountain. These cliffs look like they would offer an experienced rock climber a significant challenge! Just beyond the cliffs a short way, the shrewd observer will find the remains of an old water tank (2.1 miles) used to replenish the locomotive's steam engine. Recently the water tank was intentionally collapsed to prevent injury to road users. The tank's old location is marked on the 1986 version of the Sierra National Forest's Mt. Diablo Meridian Map as "W.T."

Those who desire a longer walk can continue 2.5 more miles to the intersection of Road 9S 03 (4.6 miles) which leads back to Musick Mountain. This spot is known as Dawn. It features a lovely meadow; one that would make a perfect picnic spot! Total time: 4 hours.

Cautions

In summer, cars and other wheeled vehicles can share the road with you. Because they are not expecting to encounter walkers or other pedestrians, be sure to give way. Except for that one caveat, I have found the area to be free of any other hazard.

Special Attractions

Beautiful views, birding, wildflowers, and history! This trail is also wheelchair accessible. With a railroad's moderate grade, chair travel to the first penstock is viable. The entire elevation drop from the start of the trail to Dawn is only 400 feet!

HIKE NUMBER 21
S J & E Railroad
Shaver Crossing to Old Cascada (Big Creek)

Category: Easy
Length: 3.2 Miles Round Trip
Time: 1.5 Hours
Map: U.S.G.S. Musick Mt. And Huntington Lake Quadrangles

Directions from Shaver Lake
Directions to this trailhead are the same as to Shaver Crossing from the previous hike. If you only want to walk three miles, you can plant a car at the other end. To do this, continue past Shaver Crossing 3.5 miles to a red garage in Old Cascada. Cascada was the original name of Big Creek.
We parked just off the road next to the old, red garage. Parking is also available 100 yards down the road near Pitman Creek.

General Description
This is a wonderful walk with a close-up view of the back of Powerhouse Number 1! Although the rush of the turbines is loud in the beginning, the sounds of nature quickly resume as you round the corner and continue toward Camp Sierra Station and Shaver Crossing. This is a safe, easy walk. It would also make a nice cross-country ski or snowshoe trip.

The Route
From the red garage on the Huntington Lake Road, head West/ Northwest down a small, almost obscure trail toward the water and the sound of Powerhouse Number 1. Descending approximately 500 feet, the railroad grade is reached. This point was the terminus of the S J & E railroad. From this spot, the train would back up across a trestle into New Cascada.
Follow the railroad grade past Dam Number 4. This dam was constructed after the first three dams were built above on Hunting-ton Lake. Continue along the grade toward the West. At 1.3 miles

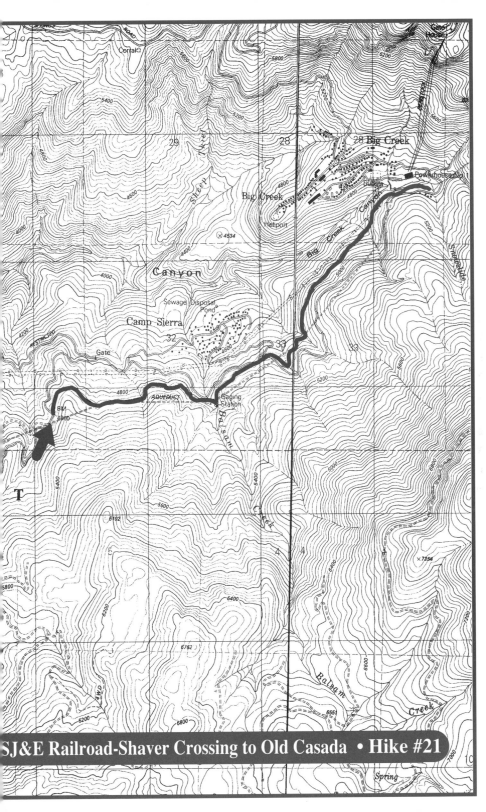

SJ&E Railroad-Shaver Crossing to Old Casada • Hike #21

the grade crosses an old trestle over Snow Slide Creek. The old trestles were never removed. They were supplanted with culverts and buried with dirt. This trestle is apparent because of the small sink holes on the road surface.

In another .3 mile, the grade meets the Huntington Lake Road at Camp Sierra Station. Cross the Huntington Lake Road and continue beyond the gate marking Forest Service road 8S 08. Just before the gate is an old Mile Post marker. This marker indicates that you are 24.6 miles from Auberry. (Marathoners take note!) Continue walking beyond the green gate toward Shaver Crossing. At 2.0 miles you will meet Balsam Creek. This water flows from Balsam Forebay above you and it supplies Camp Sierra. That is the purpose of the white PVC piping and the water tanks on the road.

Cross the old wood trestle, and continue approximately one mile to a large open logger's yarding area. From this spot the Chiquito Ridge mountains beyond Bass Lake can be seen. Foremost on the ridge is Shuteye Peak at 8,351 feet. In the other direction, Kerkoff Dome marks the east side of Big Creek.

Of historic interest, just as you leave the yarding area, on your left, near the trees, lies an old wooden pipe. The pipe was probably used as a culvert. Its remains are the wooden slats of the pipe ensconced in the wire that bound it together.

In another third of a mile, the Shaver Crossing is reached (3.2 miles).

Cautions

Few. An occasional car on the road. Ear damage from prolonged picnicking by the powerhouse. It's a stretch thinking about this one. Excessive anxiety from a hectic week at work? No Zoloff?

HIKE NUMBER 22
Red Mountain

Category: Moderate/Difficult
Length: 4 Miles Round Trip
Time: 4 Hours
Maps: U.S.G.S. Dogtooth Peak and Huntington Lake Quadrangles

Directions From Shaver Lake
From the hardware store in the middle of the village of Shaver Lake, head northeast toward Huntington Lake on Route 168. At 13.2 miles, turn right off Route 168 on the Red Mountain Trailhead Road. Follow this road for 2 miles and bear right at the intersection. Continue an additional 2.2 miles and turn left at a cattle corral. As this road becomes more and more like a horse trail, proceed 3.3 more miles to a lovely, beach-like area. This marks the intersection of the roads leading to West, Mirror, and Strawberry Lakes and the trail to Red and Coyote Lakes.

Parking
There is plenty of good parking in the vicinity of the intersection. You will be happy to leave your car/vehicle behind and to ramble off after your ride!

General Description
Red Mountain has had a special calling to me since first arriving in Shaver Lake. Visible from most all of the surrounding summits, Red Mountain stands alone, prominently displaying the red, rocky top that so distinguishes its presence.

When you arrive at the summit of Red Mountain, you will be rewarded with one of the finest views of the region attainable from any peak. In addition, because of the steep, rocky climb to the top, you will enjoy the reward of accomplishment special to this crag. Red Mountain is a true adventure!

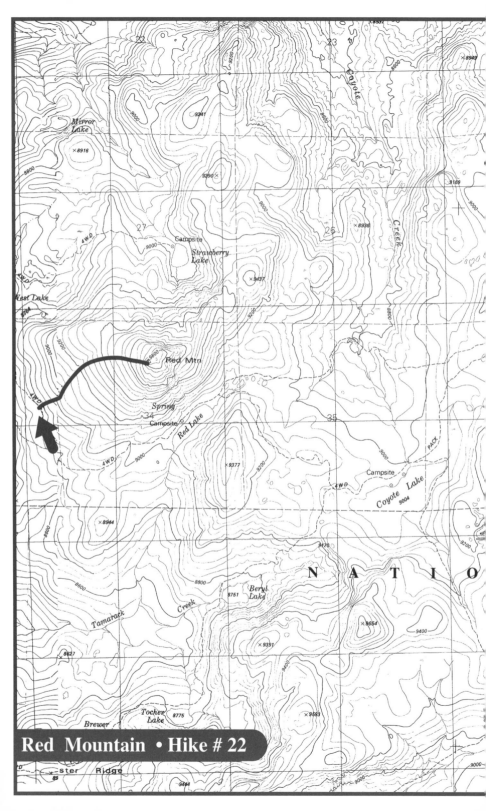

Red Mountain • Hike # 22

The Route

Upon leaving your vehicle, head right, down the Red Lake trail/ road. It looks like a road at first, but soon the trail qualities will reveal themselves. Follow this passage across a brook and back up the hill on the other side of the water. Reaching .5 miles, turn left at the tall sign marking the Red Mountain Trail. (Note: The reason that the trail sign is so tall is not to accommodate Fresno State basketball players, but to be visible to snowmobilers using the trail in the winter.)

The trail you are about to enter is really not a trail at all! Designed as a snowmobile trail, hikers were not considered in the original design. However, this route is one of the best bushwhacks you will ever find. I define a good bushwhack as one where there are few actual bushes to whack!

Follow a vague path up from the road. Your route will lead you northerly and then gradually turn more to the east. As the trail, if you will, begins to gain ground you will soon overlook a meadow to your left. This meadow contains the outlet stream from West Lake. As you continue upward, if you are along the left edge of the mountainside, you can get great views of West Lake below. Continue ever upward along the left side of some open meadows. Used as grazing land in the summer, you will find lupine, desert paintbrush, Sego lilies, and penstemon to brighten up your way! This wildflower display will continue to entertain you until you reach the base of the summit. There, beneath the peak, you will find a rare display of Golden Columbine! This virtual garden is unique to Red Mountain.

The summit may be gained many ways, but I prefer a simple, straightforward route scrambling up the middle of the mountain. This piece of the trip can be intimidating to a novice and inadvisable for young children. In case of doubt, the use of a rope is advised.

An unseen hazard in steep terrain is loose rock. A rock knocked loose from above can cause serious injury to the unsuspecting hiker below. To minimize the chance of injury, keep the group close together and try not to follow directly below the person above. Of course, a helmet is the best protection in a situation such as this.

Most hikers will find the route appealing and relatively risk free. I am mentioning the rope and helmet as the most prudent choice in situations with loose rock and steep pitches. The use of that equipment is governed by individual discretion!

Gaining the top, the views will excite you and reward you. The views of Dinkey Lakes, Kaiser Peak, and the Sierras beyond are unparalleled! Find a nice spot to rest and enjoy!

Cautions

Apart from the caveat about loose rock, the only caution is in vehicle choice for the approach. Don't bring the low rider or a car with low or loose parts. You may end up leaving some of your equipment behind.

In addition, if you are uncomfortable with route finding, this trailless trek may not be your cup of tea. This day trip is more enjoyable if you have some experience behind you, or along side of you!

Special Attractions

This is by far one of the best day trips in the Shaver Lake area. The lack of crowds (I've never seen a soul off the jeep trails), the natural beauty, and the excitement of the summit make this a wonderful trip. The summit of Red Mountain, visible from Sierra Summit and all the surrounding area, will always stand to remind you of the wonderful and exciting experience you had on your day in the mountains!

HIKE NUMBER 23
Potter Pass Cut-Off Trail

Category: Moderate
Length: 4 Miles Round Trip
Time: 2-2.5 Hours
Map: U.S.G.S. Kaiser Peak Quadrangle

Directions From Shaver Lake

From the hardware store in the center of the village of Shaver Lake, head northeast 20.4 miles to the Eastwood Visitor Center. Here, at the junction of the Kaiser Pass Road, turn right and continue up the ridge for an additional 2.8 miles to the entrance road to the Potter Pass Trail (23.2 miles). This left turn is marked by a sign bearing the trail's name.

Parking

There is ample parking near the trailhead. It appears that the Forest Service planned well for this trail's use.

General Description

This trail provides the more enterprising hiker an alternative route to Potter Pass and the lands beyond. Following the course of Potter Creek for most of the way, the lovely, gentle sounds of the creek make for a pleasant companion. Of course, depending upon the cacophony of your normal week, the sound of the creek could be a balm no matter who is accompanying you!
Another highlight of this walk is that you begin at approximately 8,000 feet. If you were from the East Coast where the tallest mountain, Mount Washington, stands at 6,288 feet, this hike's origination point would tickle you, too.

The Route

Beginning on the left side of the creek, follow the well-grooved path through a small meadow to the junction of the Huntington Lake Trail (.2 miles). Turn right toward Potter Pass.

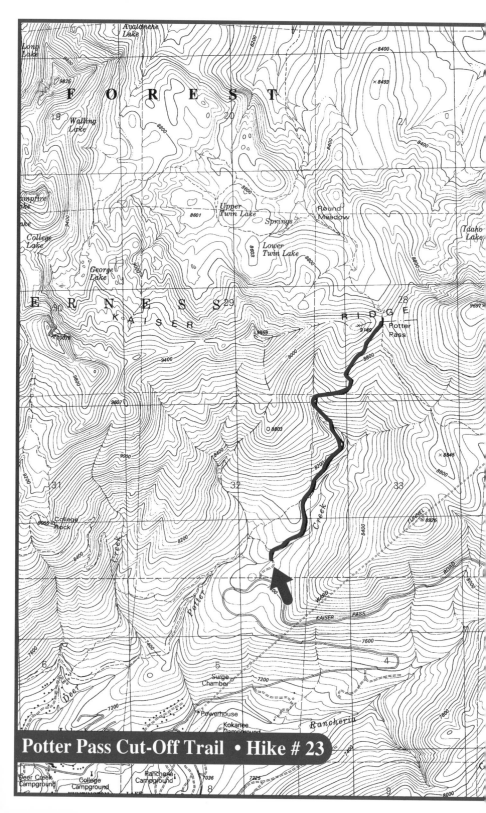

Potter Pass Cut-Off Trail • Hike # 23

Ambling gently along the creek, you will meet another trail heading left at approximately .4 miles. Stay right toward Potter Pass. The trail continues, climbing only moderately, to cross Potter Creek (.9 miles). This is a good spot for a break before beginning your ascent.

Crossing the creek, the trail challenges the hiker with a set of switchbacks slabbing up the mountain. Soon the trail brings you to a fair sized meadow and then turns right and away from the creek. Continue to climb steadily to a vista point (1.5 miles). From here you can see Sierra Summit, Red Mountain, and the Three Sisters lined up in a row!

Nearing the top, the trail slabs through a grassy, open hillside. Meeting the Potter Pass Trail (1.8 miles) stay left and continue to the pass. Marked by a large sign indicating the boundary to the Kaiser Wilderness, the pass affords spectacular views of the Northern Sierra. Prominent on the horizon are Mounts Banner and Ritter. Both 14,000-foot mountains, these peaks are on the John Muir Trail (JMT). These mountains can be reached from Tioga Pass and the upper JMT.

Cautions

Once again, I am challenged to create a caution for a lovely and, relatively gentle walk, but I will try! Look out for horses. This is a popular trail for equestrians and, upon their approach, stand downhill and stay still so as not to "spook" the horses. Although horses may seem stately and intelligent because of their awesome physical attributes, their brains are petite and their reactions, when scared, are unpredictable.

Special Attractions

The creek, the views, and the serenity of this entire walk are its special charm. Less popular than the Potter Pass Trail, your chances of encountering another hiker are remote! Consequently, your chances of seeing wildlife are enhanced! Birding is excellent along the creek, and your chances of seeing the ubiquitous Clark's Nutcracker are very good. Wildflowers, in season, are also a treat.

*Pam and Pals cruizing into Twin Lakes,
Huntington Lake section*

HIKE NUMBER 24
Potter Pass

Category: Easy
Length: 4 Miles Round Trip
Time: 2 Hours
Maps: U.S.G.S. Kaiser Peak and Mount Givens Quadrangles

Directions From Shaver Lake
From the hardware store in the middle of the village of Shaver
Lake, drive northeast approximately 20.4 miles to the Eastwood
Visitor Center at the junction of the Kaiser Pass Road. Turn right
toward Florence Lake and go 4.2 miles to the D and F Pack Station
in Badger Flat. The trailhead is directly across the road from the
pack station.

Parking
A new parking lot and outhouse await the hiker at the Potter Pass
trailhead. Three cheers for the Forest Service for this beautiful
improvement! Parking is ample and the facilities are well maintained.

General Description
This is one of the best short hikes (half-day variety) in the Sierra.
Its gentle slope and red fir forest pathway lead to one of the finest
views in the mountains.
The trail is also resplendent with great variety of wildflowers.
Asters, columbine, larkspur, paintbrush, mule ear, and penstemon
are just a few of the varieties you will encounter. Bring a flower
book for a full day of discovery.
Birders will delight, too, at the drumming sound of the Blue
Grouse. Clark's Nutcrackers and Oregon Juncos abound in the
open woods.

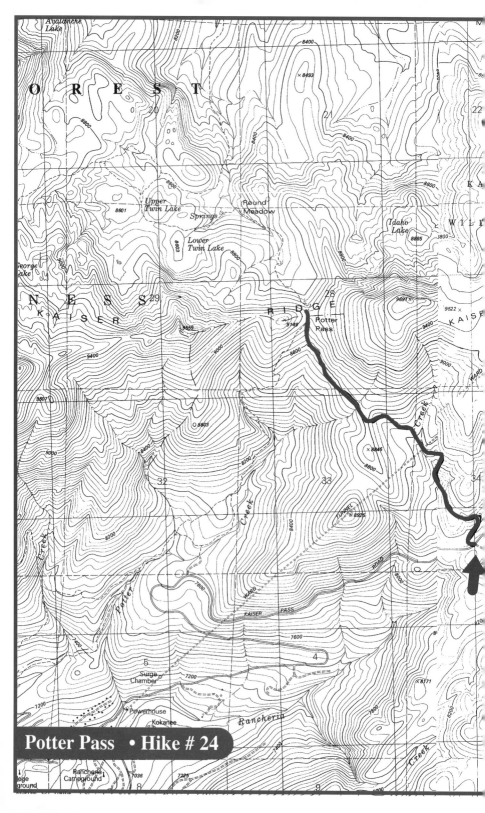

Potter Pass • Hike # 24

The Route

Starting at the north side of the Kaiser Pass Road in Badger Flat, enter the woods at the large sign marking the trailhead. Follow this clear path .28 miles to the first of the great views of the trail. Notice, also, the large juniper tree just off the trail. At .6 miles you will cross a small water source feeding a meadow below. Loaded with flowers in the mid-season, this is a good spot to begin your flower observations! In another .1 mile, a corduroy bridge leads you across a small stream. At the .9 mile mark you will cross the largest of the streams on the trail. Just across the stream, on the left, we noted larkspur.

Nearing the 1.5 mile mark, the trail turns left and enters an open meadow. The meadow was home to yellow sulfur flowers and rabbit brush. Crossing the meadow, the first views of Huntington Lake appear (1.6 miles).

Out of the woods you come onto the last of the slopes leading to your destination, Potter Pass. At exactly 2.0 miles you will meet the Potter Pass Cutoff Trail. Bear right to the col of Potter Pass. Here at 9,000 feet, behold the beauty of the views of Mount Ritter and Mount Banner. This is a great spot for a picnic or to launch off for the lakes ahead, Twin Lakes and Lake George. (See the next hike description.)

Cautions

Again, I must caution against eyestrain as you gawk at the beauty of the peaks ahead. Seriously, to contrive a caution, I would have to be creative. This is one of the most benign of the walks I have undertaken. That is what makes it such a joy!

Special Attractions

Everything that brings you out to the edge of the wilderness! Flowers, birds, views, and some wildlife are the frosting on the beautiful walk that Potter Pass provides. This is a good family experience!

Twin Lakes, Huntington Lake

HIKE NUMBER 25
George and Twin Lakes

Category: Moderate
Length: 9.4 Miles Round Trip
Time: 6 Hours
Maps: U.S.G.S. Kaiser Peak and Mt. Givens Quadrangles

Directions From the Top of Potter Pass

This hike is a continuation of either the Potter Pass Trail or the Potter Pass Cutoff. From the trail of your choice, either Potter Pass or the Potter Pass Cutoff, follow the directions in this guide from Shaver Lake to that trailhead.

General Description

This extension of the Potter Pass trip brings the hiker farther into the mountains and in direct contact with spectacular views of the north side of Kaiser Peak. The lakes also make a great destination for fishing, a foin* picnic, or just a good excuse to prolong the joy of a great mountain day!

The Route

Beginning at the top of Potter Pass, descend northerly following along the left side of the meadow below. This trail ambles along the backside of the pass and reaches the junction of the Sample Meadow Trail in .7 miles.

Turn left toward Twin Lakes. The trail slabs along revealing spectacular views of the Sierra at almost every turn! Shortly, you will reach the first of the Twin Lakes (1.2 miles). This lake was formerly titled White Cliff Lake (Three Forests Interpretive Association, 1997) because of the granite rock face on its southern shore.

After you leave the first lake, you will pass a low bog on your left. Shortly after, you will arrive on the shore of Twin Lake (1.4 miles). Circling the lake to the right, you will run into the junction of the trail to Sample Meadow (1.5 miles).

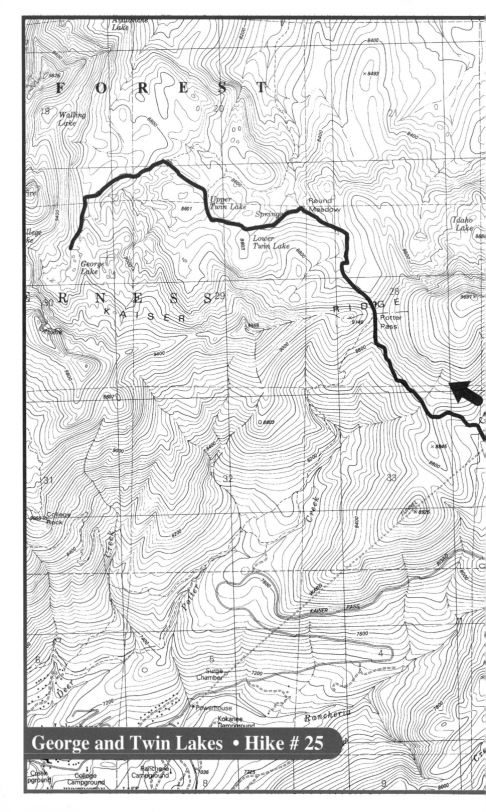

George and Twin Lakes • Hike # 25

From the trail junction, turn left toward George Lake. This trail takes you around to the back of Twin Lake. From the climb, you will gain great views of the lake below! Of note along this route are many quartz crystals you will observe. Climbing ever upward, you will soon meet the outlet stream of George Lake. Up still more, the lake is gained at 2.7 miles from Potter Pass. George Lake is quite a rewarding spot for a picnic or a photo of the backside of Mount Kaiser.

Cautions

This is a lengthy trip and, like most trips demanding of time, is best begun in the morning. Allowing ample time, the hikers can enjoy all the beauty and experience none of the hassle of rushing along!

Special Attractions

Though this trip can be great nearly anytime the road is open, I prefer October for this hike. I enjoy the aspen grove and the fall foliage show. But whenever you can experience this walk; it is worth the effort. This is one of the premier walks in the region!

* *The term foin is a Shakespearean term, and it was contributed by Dr. Eugene Zumwalt. Taken from Henry the Fourth, Part 1, Falstaff described himself as a man who would, "foin any man, woman, or child!" Dr. Zumwalt taught in the English department at Fresno State University until 1999.*

Taking a break on the trail

HIKE NUMBER 26
Mount Givens

Category: Moderate/ Difficult
Length: 6 Miles Round Trip
Time: 4 Hours
Map: U.S.G.S. Mount Givens Quadrangle

Directions from Shaver Lake

From the hardware store in the middle of downtown Shaver Lake, drive north 20.4 miles to the Eastwood Visitor Center at the junction of the Kaiser Pass Road. Turn right toward Florence and Edison Lakes and drive up the pass 6.8 miles to the height of land. Turn right and drive one mile to White Bark Vista. This is the road for which you bought your Sport Utility Vehicle.

Parking

Parking is ample at the trailhead. Because the vista also converges with the jeep road, there is not a clear stopping point. Just don't drive over the edge!

General Description

This breezy and cool summer day, I was joined by Catherine and David Nazaroff, Camp Edison campers, and Denise Bauer, Edison's recreation staff. We were excited to discover Mt. Givens and to see the great views of the Sierra that this trail provides. Most of the hike to Mt. Givens is on the Dusy Ershim jeep or OHV (off highway vehicle) trail. Although we did not see any jeeps on our walk, I could imagine the trail filled with them. If that is the case, it is possible to avoid the road and to follow a line just above along the ridge. You will do that anyway when you get close to the mountain's top. Bushwacking here is like cutting across the rough at the golf course, so missing the trail or road is not major.
I'd give this hike very high marks because of the view, altitude, and beauty of the mountain! This is a very rewarding hike!

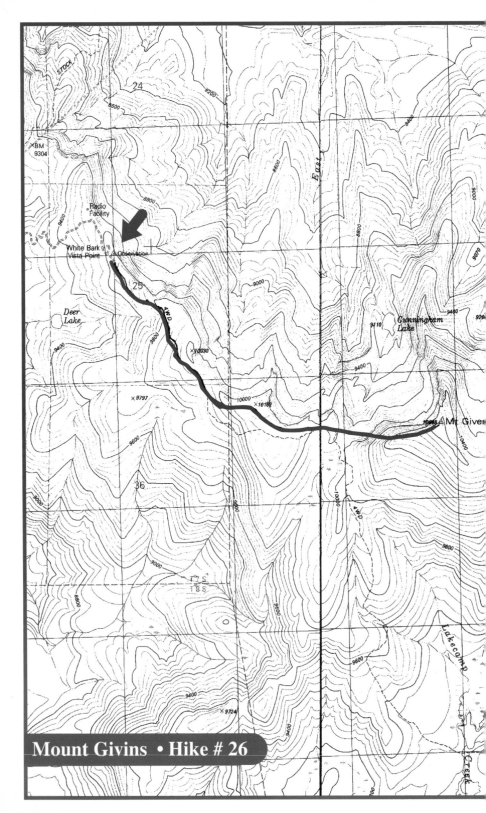

Mount Givins • Hike # 26

The Route

The trail begins at the White Bark Vista parking area and proceeds generally southeast along the ridge's crest. Crossing an open meadow lush with low lupine, there are good views of Kaiser Peak to the southwest. In .2 miles, find the entrance to the Dusy Ershim road follow its course through the woods.

At .4 miles, you will find good views of both Huntington and Deer Lake to the south. For the view enthusiast, in a short distance, you can leave the road and hike up to the left for great views of the high Sierra and Edison Lake.

In just over one mile, cross a height of land and catch the first glimpse of Mt. Givens to the northeast. Shortly, the trail will diverge left from the road and more closely follow the ridge. At 1.4 miles the trail will rejoin the jeep trail and continue to slab over the top of a small summit (10,162'). We found this spot perfect for a refuel before the final summit!

Descend to a large meadow then pass a large spire on your left. Continue and climb out of the meadow to the side of Mt. Givens. Here, at 2.3 miles, look for some slight cairns extending left up the mountain. This route has not been well trodden, so you may have difficulty going cairn or duck to mark. However, if you follow a generally eastern track, you will find the top without getting lost. Keeping toward the ridge on the left, the views will keep you refreshed as you continue to climb toward your destination!

At 3.0 miles you will gain the summit. You will know it by the electronic monitoring gear and the fact that you just can't go any higher!

Cautions

Trail finding is a bit of a challenge, but the biggest challenge is the altitude. Hiking at 10,000 feet is more than a walk in the park. Expect the thin air to stretch you a little.

Special Attractions

The largest ten thousand footer in the book! And you don't have to start at the lake to climb this one! Beginning at 9,800 feet feels like you're cheating until you've walked up and down for a couple

of miles then you'll know you earned this one! No free rides!
Of course, you will be happy to see the views of all the mountains
in the area and beyond. It makes you muse for more days in these
heavenly spaces above the valley floor.

HIKE NUMBER 27
Nellie Lake

Category: Moderate
Length: 8 Miles Round Trip
Time: 5-6 Hours
Maps: U.S.G.S. Kaiser Peak and Huntington Lake Quadrangles

Directions From Shaver Lake

From the hardware store in the heart of the village of Shaver Lake, drive northeast on Highway 168 toward Huntington Lake. Passing Sierra Summit Ski Area (18.7 miles), you will soon come to the junction of the Kaiser Pass Road and the location of the ranger station (20.4 miles). Bear left toward Huntington Lake. Follow along the lakeshore until you reach Upper Billy Creek Campground (24.9 miles). Turn right and follow the signs to the parking area.

Parking

Driving .4 miles from the turn off on the Huntington Lake Road, you will find that there is ample parking at the trailhead.

General Description

The trail to Nellie Lake is one of the finest examples of a Sierra Trail designed for pack animals and stock. Its gradual ascent treats you kindly, and the way is fairly smooth. Typical of many Sierra trails, there exists a plethora of flora and, if you are lucky, you will get to see a deer or two! This trail is also well endowed with red fir and, at the lake, a beautiful lodgepole pine stand. Of course, the highlight of the trip is your arrival at the pristine Nellie Lake. On our mid-August excursion we found snow patches to remind us of El Nino and the full array of late blooming flowers at their peak!

The Route

The trail is quite straightforward and without surprises. Leading left out from the parking area, head up from the flats to a meadow

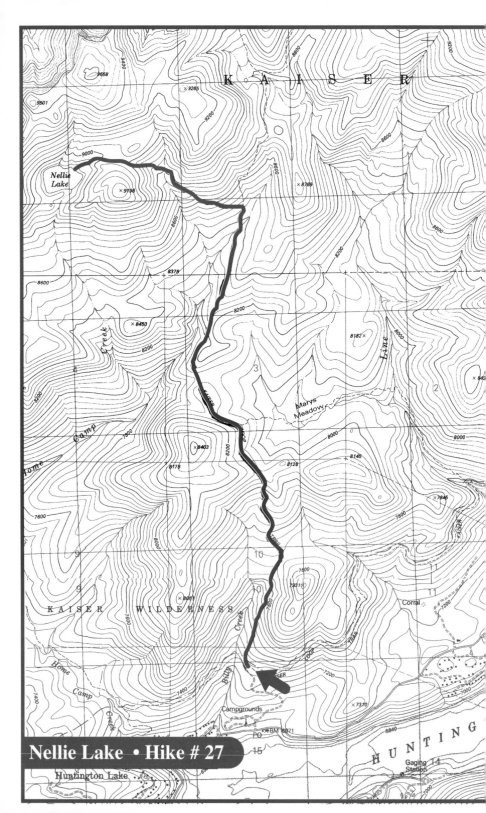

Nellie Lake • Hike # 27

(1.2 miles). Continue up along our route past the trail to Mary's Meadow, reaching a rocky outcrop just off the trail at 2.4 miles. Shortly thereafter you will pass the turnoff to Kaiser Peak (2.9 miles). Give or take an intermittent stream or two, you will ascend more dramatically and reach the height of land overlooking Nellie Lake in less than one mile. From there the trail descends to arrive on the blissful shores of your destination (4.0 miles).

Cautions
Look out for horses and the inevitable dust that follows them. As a courtesy to the equestrians, stand well off to the side of the trail and make as little distraction as possible. If you have a dog, please control them as well. Other than horse manure, I can't think of anything to spoil a walk as serene as this one.

Special Attractions
The lake is special and so is the walk to reach it. For me, one of the highs of hiking this trail is to see it as often as I do from locations in and around Shaver Lake and to feel the joy of having climbed it. The area immediately above Nellie Lake is distinguished by a rocky prominence. This mini-peak is visible on the left side of Kaiser Peak.

*Shaver, Becky, Pam & Greg on
Kaiser Peak, Huntington Lake*

HIKE NUMBER 28
Kaiser Peak's College Rock

Category: Moderate
Length: 6 Miles Round Trip
Time: 3 Hours
Map: U.S.G.S. Kaiser Peak Quadrangle

Directions From Shaver Lake

From the hardware store in the center of the village of Shaver Lake, drive 20.1 miles north on Highway 168 toward Huntington Lake. At the junction of the Kaiser Pass Road, stay left toward Rancheria. Pass the restaurant and bar and turn right at 21.0 miles. This road is marked with a pack station sign in season. Follow the road to the pack station.

Parking

Park in the parking area on the left at the end of the access road. If the steel gate on the road leading to the pack station is locked, park at the side of the road below the gate.

General Description

This is the first half of the climb to the summit of Kaiser Peak. However, in itself, this is a classic hike. It features all of the beautiful views one would ever desire. Overlooking Huntington Lake, the College Rock hike affords unparalleled photographs of the lake and the mountains immediately surrounding the area: China Peak, Red Mountain, and Black Butte. Beginning at an altitude of 7,200 feet, this trail ascends to 9,100 feet in a distance of 3.0 miles. All in all, a great hike!

The Route

Beginning at the back of the pack station, follow the signs leading toward College Rock and the summit of Kaiser Peak. This trail is well marked and quite easy to follow.

After slabbing up the first half mile, you will find the first of many

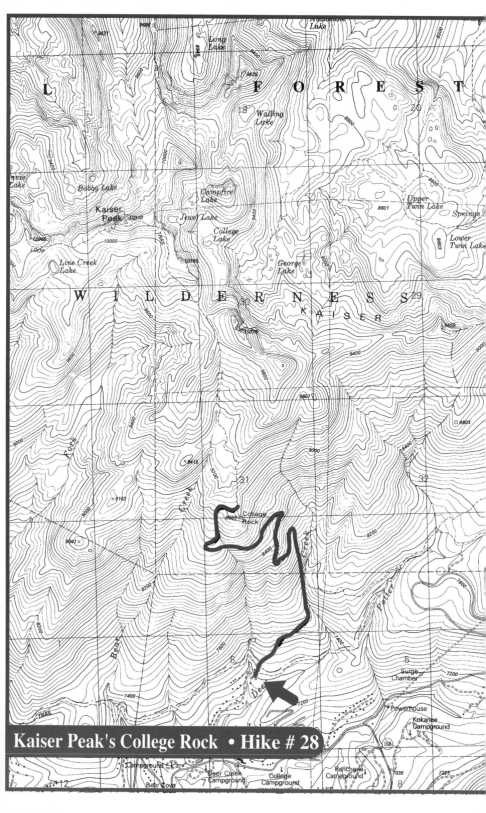

Kaiser Peak's College Rock • Hike # 28

views of the lake. This glimpse is directly across a glacial erratic, a large boulder deposited in its present location by the receding glacier ten thousand years ago!

Continuing along, the trail joins a small stream and follows its course for a quarter of a mile or so. At the 1.23-mile mark, you will find a sharp bend in the trail marked by a very interesting granite monument artfully eroded by melting glacial ice. This spot makes a great rest stop and photo opportunity! You have now climbed 900 feet!

Climbing on, you will continue to encounter beautiful vistas every one half mile or so. The finest of the views comes at 2.2 miles. Here the view of the lake is worth another stop and photo! In another .8 miles, after winding your way up through the red fir forest, you will reach the top of College Rock. This spot is named for the annual destination of Fresno State students in their early twentieth century outings to Kaiser Peak.

Cautions

Other than getting locked inside the steel gate at the access road, there are very few cautions for this hike. The trail is well marked and the slopes, designed for horses, are not steep. This should be regarded as a serious hike and not just a walk. It is more fun with conditioning and a good supply of water!

Special Attractions

Views, views, and views! We also saw several deer and a golden eagle on our walk. Expect wild flowers in season and beautiful surroundings!

Shaver, Becky & Pam on
Kaiser Peak, Huntington Lake

HIKE NUMBER 29
Kaiser Peak

Category: Difficult
Length: 10.6 Miles Round Trip
Time: 6-8 Hours
Map: U.S.G.S. Kaiser Peak Quadrangle

Directions From Shaver Lake
Follow the directions for the preceding hike to College Rock.

Parking
Again, these directions are the same as for the hike to College Rock.

General Description
Beginning at the College Rock, this route takes the ambitious hiker to the 10,300-foot summit to Kaiser Peak! Climbing above the Twin Lakes high above tree line, the views of the Central Sierras are unbeatable! This is the crown jewel hike of the region. Those who reach the peak will be greatly rewarded! The route is spectacular, and this trip has become my annual favorite.

The Route
These distances are marked as cumulative from the base of the College Rock Trail.

Beginning at 9,100 feet, at the top of College Rock, follow the trail as it leads you ever upward toward the vast expanse of mountain ahead. At 3.6 miles (9,440 feet), you will cross a meadow of willow laced with small rivulets in the spring.

Heading still upward, you will climb out of the trees at 4.3 miles and get your first glimpses of the high mountain. This delicate lupine and plant kingdom experiences some of the harshest conditions plants can withstand. Almost Arctic in climate, the high mountain plants and trees have to be especially hardy to survive! At 4.5 miles, you will have descended to the col that looks over

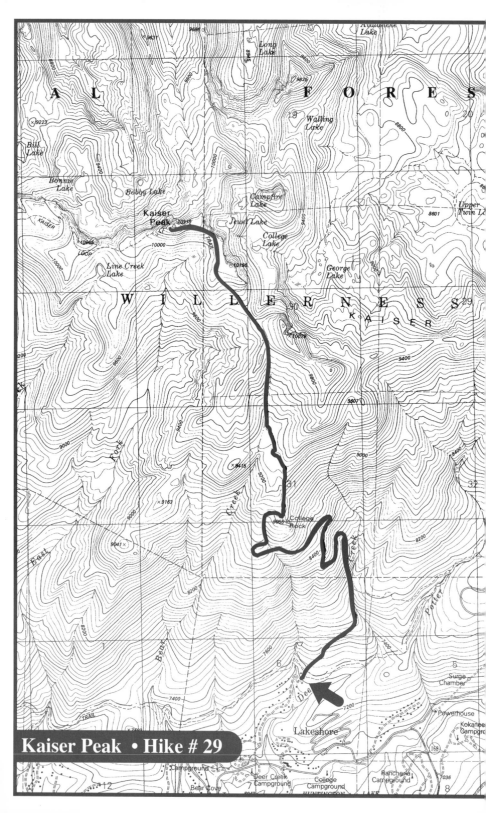

Kaiser Peak • Hike # 29

Twin Lakes and Lake George. There you will also find views of Mounts Ritter and Banner in the Adam's Wilderness. Slabbing upward along the long side of the mountain, you will reach a height of land (4.8 miles). You now finish the ascent of the last one half mile with breathtaking views. The 360-degree view from the summit is the best in the area! This climb is without peer in the Huntington/Shaver Lake region!

Cautions

Bring lots of warm clothes, sun block, and extra food and water for the long trek. This is a real mountain, and there are no amenities until you reach the bottom!

Special Attractions

This entire trek is a special attraction. Don't forget your camera and field glasses! There is a lot to please the eye!

Andy & Betty on a foothill Conservancy hike

HIKE NUMBER 30 AND 31
Mystery Lake/Dinkey Lakes Loop

Category: Easy/Moderate
Length: 2.5-6.0 Miles Round Trip
Time: 2-5 Hours
Map: U.S.G.S. Dogtooth Peak Quadrangle

Directions From Shaver Lake
From the junction of Route 168 and the Dinkey Creek Road, head east toward Dinkey Creek. At 8.9 miles, turn left on to Rock Creek Rd. Drive along Rock Creek for 5.9 miles. Turn right. Drive 4.6 miles to a sharp right turn that reverses your direction and takes you 2.2 miles to the trailhead for Dinkey Lakes. The total distance and driving time from Shaver Lake is 21.6 miles in 45-60 minutes, depending upon the respect that you have for your car and passengers.

Parking
As you come down the final hill to the trailhead, stay to the left and the parking area will reveal itself to you. There is ample parking; however, the problems of break-ins attendant with wilderness parking are present here, too. Be sure not to leave valuables and coolers in eyesight.

General Description
The Dinkey Lakes area affords a great variety of experiences ranging from a family picnic/hike to Mystery Lake (1.0 mile) to extended overnight backpacks. Related activities in this region cover diversity from fishing to mountaineering. The Dinkey Lakes area is surrounded by the Three Sisters and Dogtooth peaks (10,302 feet). All of these summits are over 10,000 feet. Wherever one gazes, beautiful views abound! Of the many days logged in this region, the day I'm recalling while writing this description contained the most spectacular display of wildflowers that I have

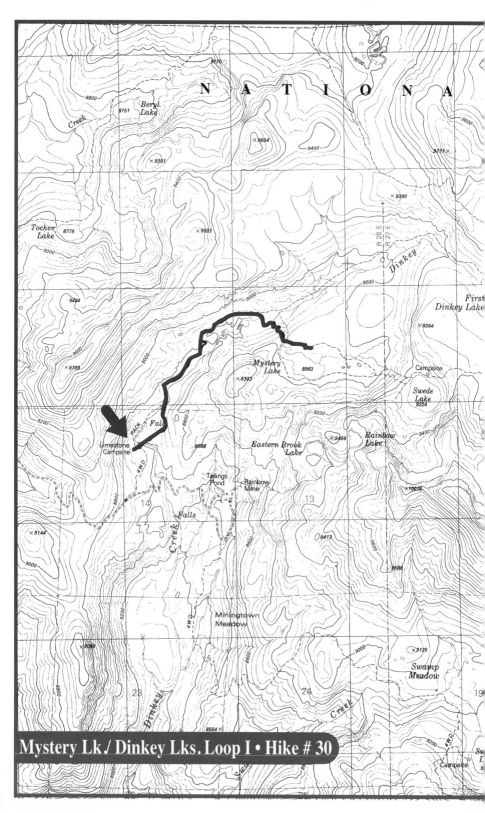

Mystery Lk / Dinkey Lks. Loop I • Hike # 30

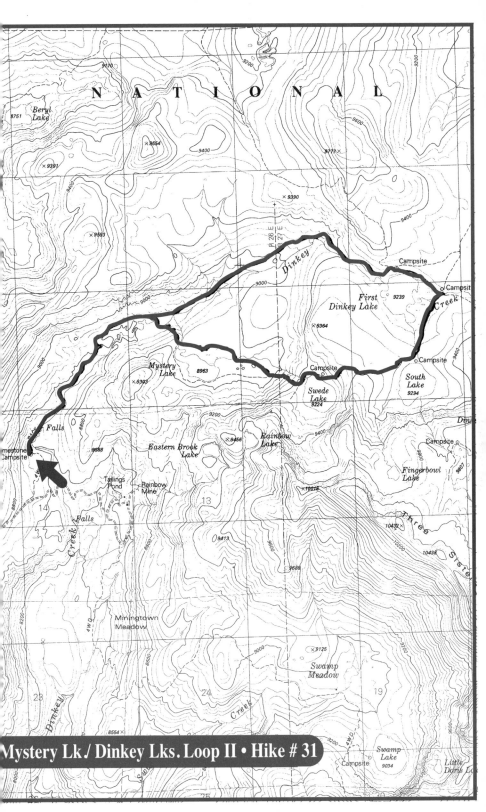

Mystery Lk./ Dinkey Lks. Loop II • Hike # 31

seen to date. On the shore of the First Dinkey Lake there must have been one million Shooting Stars. We also saw Columbine, Lilies, Desert Paintbrush, Sego Lilies, and others too numerous for me to identify!

The Route

Beginning at the parking lot, the trailhead leaves to the right. The beginning is clearly marked by a large sign. The trail descends gradually to Dinkey Creek and crosses the creek almost immediately. On the other side of the creek, bear right up the hill. In a short distance (less than a 0.5 mile), the trail again crosses Dinkey Creek and follows its course approximately 0.5 mile more to the junction of the Mystery Lake and the First Dinkey Lake trails (1 mile). Turning right, the trail leads over Dinkey Creek and slabs left up a singular and gradual switchback to the outflow of Mystery Lake (1.3 miles). For anyone seeking an enjoyable hour or so hike, this one is tough to beat!

Continuing from Mystery by circling left around the lake, the trail challenges the hiker with a rigorous ascent to Swede Lake (2.0 miles). Climbing to a height of 9,200 feet, you will have ascended approximately 600 feet from the parking lot; however, most of that climb occurred in the last 0.5 mile!

From Swede Lake, follow the trail to the left hiking up to the height of land overlooking South Lake. South Lake (2.5 miles) makes a nice destination for lunch or an overnight stay. The falls on the opposite side of the lake provide an auditory balm for those weary of city sounds.

The trail leaves South Lake near the outflow stream and meanders down to First Dinkey Lake (3.0 miles). The old trail to First Dinkey followed this stream to the meadow and turned right to meet the trail descending from Second Dinkey Lake. However, because of damage to the meadow and wet conditions in spring, a new trail has been rerouted above the old one. This fact is hard to grasp as your eye and inertia will tend to carry you past this subtle turn in the trail down toward First Dinkey. All I can say is keep your eyes peeled!

When you meet the trail from the high lakes, turn left and follow the route along the lakeshore to the outlet stream. Here thousands of wildflowers abound and views of the Three Sisters are incomparable! Follow the Dinkey Creek back down the trail to the parking lot (6.0 miles) and the cool, refreshing beverage you had foresight to leave for this moment.

Cautions
Frankly, it is hard to think of any on this trip. Let's see. Eye strain from scenic splendor? No. I would say the only cautions relate to the high peaks surrounding the lakes. Attempt these scrambles only if you are an experienced and well-equipped mountaineer. Otherwise, the trails are well marked and the routes around the lakes fairly free of obstacles. Early in the season, expect to encounter lots of snow and possibly an auto-inaccessible trailhead. Late in the season be cautious of early winter storms.

Special Attractions
As you begin the trip, if you leave the parking lot and hike to the left along Dinkey Creek, you will find a waterfall that those following the trail to the right will miss. This falls is quite spectacular in the spring, and you can avoid two crossings of the Dinkey Creek using this way. However, be cautioned that this trail is not maintained and it has its wet and muddy spots, too!
Because this is a nationally established wilderness area, it has unique protections to help retain its natural beauty. Please help maintain the character of this area by leaving only your footprints and taking only photographs and trash left behind by the less vigilant.

Twin Lake, Huntington Lake

Florence Lake & Blaney Meadows

The Florence Lake area affords those willing to drive the extra miles (13) a special reward. Located as far into the Sierra Nevada as it is possible to drive, Florence Lake is the mid-point of the John Muir Trail and a great starting point for backpackers.

Florence Lake is another area rich in history. Completed on September 11, 1926, the Florence Lake dam created the lake we know today. Shortly after the dam was completed, Fred Ross discovered and fell in love with Blaney Meadow, a large open grassland west of the lake. Fortunately, his story has been preserved and it is included in this edition to inform the reader of this areas history. The Ross family continues to operate a pack station and an Elder Hostel at Blaney. If you are lucky, you will meet one of the family members on your way in or out of the Sierras. They'll be flattered to know you read Fred's story, and you may even get to peek further into the life of the past.

Fred Ross' Memoirs

In August 1932, my good friend Harold Miller invited me to help him move 16 burros from Tuolumne Meadows, Yosemite National Park, to Tollhouse, California on foot via the John Muir Trail. The burros had been used by a group of nationally chosen Eagle Scouts who had worked in the Yosemite backcountry all summer. Harold had been chosen as one of the 16. Among other tasks they had inventoried backcountry lakes and streams for species and approximate numbers of fish populations.

They had camped out for about six weeks and had used burros to move from camp to camp. Their last camp and the end of the expedition was at Tuolumne Meadows. The "boys" on the trip were chosen by the National Park Service. I do not know what basis was used to select them, but they were all Eagle Scouts and from the western states. The National Park Service had hauled the burros in a 1929 Ford flat bed truck from John Medley's place on Lodge Road near Tollhouse. They barely made the trip to

Yosemite in the four-cylinder flat bed truck.

At the end of the expedition, Harold had volunteered to walk the burros via the "new" John Muir Trail back to the winter pasture at Tollhouse. The cost would be a two-weeks supply of food for four people. Harold chose me as one of the four and I was accepted even though I was not one of the original group. The four of us were Harold Miller, Fred Bacon, Allen Moses, and myself.

We left in early August and spent a week or more traveling to upper Bear Creek and then over Selden Pass and down to Blayney Meadows. It was my turn that day to travel behind the string and I developed a bad nosebleed coming down from Sallie Keyes. We missed the turn off of the Muir Trail and ended up at John Shipp's place. I washed up at the small pool on the hillside and was very surprised that it was hot water. The burros were loose and all over the hillside above Shipp's cabin.

John Shipp, "Doc" Earl Coleman, Maude Shipp, Dr. Thomas, Sallie Keyes Shipp, and Bill and Gertrude Berryhill were all there at the cabin watching us try to gather up our animals and start them up the canyon to Palute Creek where we camped that night.

The next morning we pushed on up the canyon to Martha Lake where there was good pasture. As we passed the Hell-For-Sure trail, we met a herd of 75 horses belonging to the Medley brothers from Tollhouse. They had been pastured in the upper canyon for the summer of 1932.

We camped at a large split rock very near the outlet of Martha Lake where there was a good fireplace and shelter under a naturally sculptured white-bark pine. We climbed Mt. Goddard the next day and enjoyed a clear 360° view for many miles. After gathering the burros early the next morning, we continued our trip and followed the Hell-For-Sure trail over the pass and into Red Mountain Basin where we established our camp at the second lake above the Punch Bowl. We stayed here two nights and were adopted by a "lost" sheep dog we named Gunga-Din. I spent the next day with the dog hiking completely around the basin from the west side of the Punch Bowl, up the south ridge and around to the pass we had crossed the day before and to the top of the nearly 11,000 foot peak of Red Mountain. We returned to camp via a long arc to the northwest and south across the basin to the Punch Bowl again. It was a long, strenuous and very enjoyable trip. That evening we had a great fish dinner from this fine chain of lakes. The next day we packed up and continued on down from the west side of the Punch Bowl and eventually camped at Long Meadow on our way to the Ranger Station at Dinky Creek. The route was through thick forests interspersed by meadows. We eventually came to a Forest Service road which led us to Dinky Creek where we camped near the Ranger Station. Jim Poor was the ranger and his wife was a former school teacher in North Fork where Harold Miller had her in elementary school. This was our first contact with "civilization" since leaving Tuolumne Meadows.

The next day was very eventful. The trail toward Tollhouse from Dinky Creek was mostly in dense forest and led south and west across the upper reaches of Blue Canyon. In crossing this canyon in deep forest and brush, we noticed some smoke rising from the lower canyon where it joins the Kings River. We hadn't gone far when we could see and smell that it must be a large fire. It actually raced up the canyon with a roar. Less than an hour later, we looked back and could see it had consumed our trail and continued on up north. It also spread toward the west and eventually became a very major wildfire.

We continued on west and the trail became a logging road which passed Peterson's mill. Shortly we met a truck convoy full of men and equipment ready to fight the fire. They stopped us and recruited us on the spot—no excuses accepted!

We unpacked our burros and put all our supplies and equipment on one of the trucks and went back toward the fire with them. The burros were turned loose and went on down the road. We wondered if we would ever see them again!

The truck convoy continued back up the "road" with us, our supplies and equipment, and probably as many as 100 men picked up by the U.S. Forest Service in the Fresno Court House Park and "conscripted" like we were to help fight fire.

We soon stopped at a place near Peterson's Mill where there were many more trucks, equipment and men setting up a fire camp—hopefully far enough west to be out of the range of the roaring fire.

It was amazing to see how quickly a kitchen was set up, space cleared and made fire safe for eventually over 400 men to occupy and sleep on the ground. We were fed a very generous lunch with piles of fresh fruit and bread and probably 50+ gallons of excellent soup. We were amazed at the organization of the Forest Service and the quick way everyone was assigned to a small ten-man crew with a Forest Serviceman in charge. We were each given a canteen of water, a "McCloud" tool, shovel and axe to use. Some of the men were paired off with long felling saws. (This was long before chain saws were developed!)

All of us were put in different crews—each with a U.S. Forest Service person as a leader. My crew was assigned a work time from 5 p.m. until 9 a.m. the next morning including "portal-to-portal" travel to the fire line.

We walked for about 1_ or 2 hours before reaching our assigned place on the fire line. It was getting dark now and the fire was slowly creeping along—sometimes with fierce bursts as it consumed a large tree. We replaced a similar crew which had started to clear a fire line some distance from the actual fire.

The goal was to completely surround the fire with a 6 to 10 foot fire line cleared down to mineral earth. Most burnable material was thrown in toward where the fire would be in a short time. This helped to slow its progress but several times a burning tree would fall across the line and we would have to back up and make a new line.

This routine continued for four days when the fire was declared contained and we were gradually "decommissioned" and dismissed. There were many tall burning snags left which had to be felled into the burned area. This was done very skillfully by several crews of Arizona Indians who were specialists at this job. It was amazing to see them in action, walking out a ways into the still smoldering area behind the fire line and in minutes without a pause in their saw strokes fell a back into the burning area.

For many Depression Era men, it was a blessing to be employed as fire fighters with all you could eat of fresh valley fruit and vegetables as well as a hearty basic hot meal (the same menu five times each 24 hours)! The pay was 20¢ an hour.

In the last days after containment sometimes someone desperate for work and wages would actually put a shovel of coals across the fire line to keep it going!

An incident along the fire line as it cooled down may be of interest. One man was very tired; the fire was calmed down in our area and our section of the fire trail was clear and completed. He lay down in a depression in the fire trail and, being very tired, fell asleep stretched out along the trail. A smoldering 12 foot pine was still burning well within the fire line. As time went on, it burned clear through at the base and it fell directly across the depression with the sleeping man. Because of the depression in the trail, the tree trunk did not touch him, but a snag of a branch tore his ear off as it fell. Needless to say, it woke him up. He had no other injuries and was able to hike out after a compress was applied to his head. A close call, and a very lucky man he was.

At last our ten-man crew was dismissed and "paid off" with script which was later converted to cash. Within two hours, the four of us tracked our burros through the unburned forest and many small meadows along the present Peterson Mill Road. We packed them up back at the fire camp and were on our way again down to the Tollhouse Road where the present fire station is. We used the "old" Tollhouse Road to bring them down to Lodge Road and to John Medley's place for the winter pasture on the hillside south and west of Lodge Road (including the area behind what is now the Sierra High School).

Harold's father, John Miller, planned to meet us at John Medley's. He was a former U.S. Forest Service ranger and later was in charge of bark-beetle control research. His office was at Stanford University where he and several graduate students held forth high in the attic in one of the Quad Buildings.

The Medley family had been in the Tollhouse area for several generations, but John lived alone now after he split up from his wife, Mary. (The "House Mother" in later years where Linda and Penny boarded while attending Sierra High.)

John lost his right lower arm in a gun accident. He had a stub below the right elbow which he used to help with his needs. At his place at the table, he had a spike driven up through the table which he used very skillfully as a hold down to help with eating cantaloupe, buttering bread, etc.

We turned the burros loose in John's pasture and stayed overnight at his place. Harold Miller's father came down to pick us up and we went to U.S. Forest Service headquarters at North Fork where my 1923 Studebaker touring car awaited. And so home again to Palo Alto.

Summer 1933

[Addendum: Richard Ross-The following account is based on a number of conversations with my dad over the years.]

In the summer of 1933, Dad participated in a joint Park Service/ U.S. Bureau of Entomology survey that traveled from Big Meadows in Sequoia Park down to Kenoyers in Cedar Grove and north on the Muir Trail to Yosemite Park. Primarily because of his experience the previous summer with the Park Service burros, Dad was taken on as one of the "packers." The trip was memorable not just because of the opportunity to revisit the high country, but because Theodore Solomons accompanied the group as a guest. Dad treasured the memory of traveling through the Evolution country with the man who had named many of the surrounding peaks and listening to his stories around the evening fire. Later, while traveling through Bear Creek, both Solomons and Dad were in a party that climbed the Seven Gables. In 1966, while climbing that peak with a group of our family and friends, Dad spoke about that earlier climb. He recalled that in 1933, Theodore Solomons mentioned to the group that when he had climbed the mountain in 1894, they had climbed the shorter peak to the north rather than the peak that is now considered the top.

1934

Bill and Gertrude Berryhill lived in Auberry where their "ranch" was at the intersection of the Auberry Road and the canyon fork which connected with the Tollhouse road a few miles below (where Canyon Fork Market is now). They pastured their herd of horses and a few burros here in the winter and had established a small pack station at Florence Lake. They had an arrangement with John Shipp to pack campers to Blayney Meadows and use his meadow campsites. They also spot packed with horses.

The burros we left at John Medley's were owned by the National Park Service. During the winter they sold them and the Berryhills got quite a few of them for their pack string. I made arrangements with the Berryhills to rent four burros for six weeks starting in August 1934. I organized a small group (four boys) and we left *early* in the morning and got to Fresno in daylight. (The cut off at Madera was not recommended.) We continued on up to Tollhouse and struggled up the unpaved Tollhouse grade. Some places the three boys got out and walked and sometimes pushed. Then on up past Shaver and through Big Creek. It took several tries to get up the steep part of this grade to Huntington Lake.

Next it was a continued struggle to get up to Kaiser Pass over the very narrow, steep road with lots of loose rocks and eventually to Jackass Meadow below the dam where we camped for several days. Harry "Bill" Berryhill and his wife, Gertrude, ran a pack station here. During the years 1932 and 1933, the lake was *completely* empty and the river ran directly into the tunnel.

We rented four burros for I think three weeks from the Berryhills and made trips into Hutchinson Meadow, Sallie Keyes, Upper Bear Creek, Evolution, and Martha L., where we climbed Mt. Goddard. We also climbed Mt. Humphreys, Mt. Senger, the Hermit, Pilot Knob, Ward Mountain, and probably others.

The burros we used were from the same group of 16 which I had helped return them from Tuolumne to John Medley's during the summer of 1932. They included Dago, Rum, Gandhi, and Sandy. I was pleased to see and use them again.

Blayney Meadows was leased for pasture and camping by the Berryhills from John Shipp. There were many camps established along the west side of the river across from John Shipp's cabin. Also, there were about eight or ten sites at lower Blayney and some along the trail near Sallie Keyes and Senger Creek. I would judge there to be 50 to 75 people camped in the Blayney Meadows area *all summer and fall* during the 1930s.

The main packing business was from the road's end at Florence Lake to Blayney Meadows. Animals would be scheduled *daily* to pack people down from Blayney and another party would be met around noon to 2 p.m. to be packed into Blayney. This was a daily routine with a full schedule going and coming all summer into September and October. They had about 25 head including ten burros. The burros were rented for walking trips and horses were used for spot packing mostly to Blayney Meadows.

People in those days rarely had special camping gear and supplies. The gear they had was bulky, heavy, and not always suited to pack easily or comfortably on an animal. Very few people rented animals to ride—it was too expensive and these were mid-Depression years. The rates were as follows:

Burros	$1.00/day	100 lbs. Pack
Horses	$2.00/day	150 lbs. Pack
Packer	$2.00/day	$2.00 for his
Horse		
Grazing on U.S. Forest Service Land		$2.00/animal/
		month horses & mules
		$1.00/animal/
		month burros

Most parties made a base camp and hiked and fished at nearby lakes and streams. There were a few back packers, but most of them made their own pack sacks or boards. That is what we did and somehow we were able to do quite well with homemade things *and a few burros* to help out so we could move around and stay longer in the mountains.

The first year we rented burros from the Berryhills was 1934, when I invited Lloyd Wilson, Ernie Wuthmann, David MacKenzie, and Bob Buss. We made a four-week trip from mid-July to mid-August. We made equipment and gathered supplies and food in Palo Alto. My father constructed a dehydrator from a University of California agriculture plan and much time was spent preparing various vegetables and some fruit and meat. It was a long process to dehydrate foods. Vegetables were "blanched" in boiling water after being pealed and sliced about _" thick and then spread out carefully on the trays of the dehydrator. Every few hours the trays would be shifted so the food would be dried more evenly. A hundred pound sack of potatoes weighed about ten pounds when dried!—but the bulk was not reduced much because the slices would shrink and curl. We experimented with all vegetables but potatoes, peas, corn, and carrots turned out best.

In July 1934, after a stint as a leader at the Boy Scouts of America camp in Swanton, north of Santa Cruz, three of us struggled up to Florence Lake. After camping and exploring around Jackass Meadow and getting used to the altitude, we rented four burros for a month. We camped for several nights at the public camp near the hot springs and then took off up the John Muir Trail to Mammoth Lakes where we met Bob Buss and his family by prearrangement. Bob came back with us to Blayney Meadows where we re-supplied from things we had left with the Berryhills and then took off up Paiute Creek to Hutchinson Meadow for a base camp. During the next week we explored the canyons, glaciers, and climbed Pilot Knob and Mt. Humphrey.

We returned to Blayney Meadows and re-supplied from our cache at Florence Lake in the old Studebaker and took off to see Evolution and to climb several of the high peaks and the Hermit. After climbing and exploring in the Evolution Valley and Basin, we returned again to re-supply from the old 1923 Studebaker at Florence Lake and this time we went up Goddard Canyon, camped at Martha Lake and climbed the mountain. On our way back, we went over Hell-For-Sure Pass and camped at the second lake above the Punch Bowl for a few days and then returned to Blayney Meadows and a hot bath.

We returned to Florence Lake and after having had a wonderful, adventurous trip with burros, returned to Palo Alto in the faithful old 1923 Studebacker.

1935

During the winter, we planned another trip to the mountains and again arranged for the Berryhill burros. This time we were invited to make a base camp which was where the Mackenzie camp and cabin are now. Their pole corral was in the grove behind their cabin where the trail now goes to the Muri Trail Ranch. In the spring of 1935, we prepared equipment to be hauled up to Blaney for more substantial accommodations in what became a base camp for yearly summer packs into the surrounding valleys and canyons and mountains. We gradually made improvements and conveniences so we could operated more efficiently and have a home base. We built the tree house for storage and a rock fireplace and a base for an old wood stove which we hauled up on poles between two burros from Florence Lake. The poles were originally cut in the "Cony Camp" area where a stretcher was made to haul Lila Lofberg (the dam tender's wife) out with a broken leg. They were left on the bank of the Florence Lake where the bridge is now. They came across in a boat to pick up Lila after a four-day trip to "Cony Camp" to immobilize her leg and bring her out slowly on a stretcher attached to the saddle of one of the burros. We used two burros to haul the stove up in one day.

We built a small enclosed area near the large lodge pole with the 1935 sign on it. We cleared some brush, put up a pole enclosure, a lean-to frame for a canvas, a fireplace backing and a rock-lined path down to the river nearby. The horse drive every morning came up across the island where we now have cabins and across the river to a corral in the woods behind where Alec's cabin is now—our first construction in Blayney Meadows!

We put in a hitching rail along the east side of the compound. Two pole frames were built to stretch auto cover tarps for sleeping lean-tos. At the end of the season most things were carefully packaged and stored in the tree house cache. We were very happy to be here and the Berryhills were very glad to have close neighbors. It made it much more convenient to re-supply food for pack trips up here rather than the long trip down and around the lake for re-supply. This spot at Blayney Meadows became a base camp for many following summer hiking and animal pack trips.

John Shipp claimed ownership of all of upper Blayney Meadows and we rented our site from him. We paid, I think, $1.00 per week per person for the use of this base campsite.

190

For the next several years, we had small groups of boys from the Palo-Alto-Stanford-Los Altos area for two weeks at a time. We used Spikes Camp as a base for supplies, getting used to the altitude, learning some camping and hiking basics and day trips and hot baths up the river.

For one week after getting used to the altitude and overcoming blisters, non-efficient dish washing, packing burros and personal back packs, we went on a burro-assisted trip to Bear Creek, upper Paiute Creek, Evolution-Goddard Canyon, etc. (not all in the same trip). We fished, climbed mountains, explored side canyons and enjoyed wilderness camping, exploring, rustic construction, campfires, burros packing, and much, much more.

Since I was now in college, and the fall quarter didn't begin until almost October, I was able to stay later in the season to help the Berryhills with their pack business. These were busy times with almost daily trips to Florence Lake to meet or return many parties. Much of the time it was a daily routine to gather animals, feed and saddle and pack a party out from Blayney and around the lake. With few exceptions, most of the people walked out and in. Most of the time I made a daily trip with up to ten burros to and from the lake. Bill and Gertrude Berryhill and their packer, John Marvin, would use the horses. The Florence Lake corral was among some willows where the new paved parking area (near present SCE gate) is and a tent platform was up where the H-S headquarters is now, which was used to fix meals and stay overnight sometimes.

Blayney Meadows Sold

I'm not sure which winter it was that John Shipp sold his property to Jack Dusy—probably 1939-1940. Jack used to run a resort at Dinky Creek called "Dusys" and had a stock rental corral, cabins, campsites, and a store. It was a very popular and well used enterprise.

We called on Jack Dusy that spring to explain our use of Blayney Meadows and try to arrange use of Lost Valley Camp site as a base headquarters for our back packing and burro trips. He was friendly but non-committal about us continuing to use a part of Blayney Meadows. He had not personally been there yet and bought what he thought was the whole valley.

Mrs. Berryhill told us John Shipp had a brother who owned fifty percent of the private property at Blayney Meadows. He, George, still had property there but did not use it because of a falling out with his brother which started in 1925. This tip by Gertrude Berryhill was a turning point in our saga of Blayney Meadows.

Sometime in the late 1800s, George and John Shipp acquired several hundred acres at Blayney Meadows, Double Meadows, hillside meadow areas from just below the Tombstone as far as the meadows of upper Senger Creek and around Sallie Keyes Lakes. The total was quite a few hundred acres.

The Swamp and Overflow Act of 1852 provided opportunities for ranchers in the west to survey and file on public lands suitable for grazing and subject to later survey verification by the U.S. Lands Office that the land was indeed swampy or subject to frequent spring and storm flooding.

Up to the time of the Swamp and Overflow Act, it was often a free-for-all in the spring for valley ranchers to walk their animals (sheep, cattle, horses, and mules) to the mountain meadows. John and George Shipp were partners in the establishment of a cattle (and sometimes sheep) camp at Blayney Meadows. Their father apparently used it before turning it over to the boys.

The land had been surveyed by a Mr. Atwood, a professional surveyor who established a company of many surveyors. Mr. A did not personally do the surveying, but the original survey papers are in Fresno County with his name mentioned as the responsible state approved surveyor.

All surveying of property in California was based on the work of William H. Brewer (see "Up and Down California" 1864-1865). He was a professor at Cornell and made a trip as a botanist to California to accompany the survey team responsible for a basic, accurate survey of all of California. They started in San Francisco at the beach where they established a zero elevation point of beginning and slowly worked their way down the bay and up the east side of Oakland and then on up to the top of Mt. Diablo. This was a long slow process with mercury barometers which must be held upright at all times and checked several times against the records of a stationary barometer. It was an involved and slow to coordinate all of the data.

They established Mt. Diablo, and in the south Mt. San Jacinto as basic zero-zero reference points for the original accurate mapping of California. Their records began the range and township system of mapping and accurate recording of all property in California. Our property at Blayney Meadows is recorded as the NE_-SE_-SECTION 15-T8S-R28E of Mt. Diablo Base and Meridian. The "Whitney Survey" began in the early 1860s and was not completed officially until 1925 on our area. Between those two dates it was allowed for private surveyors with proper credentials to be hired to check on "swamp and overflow" land and register it in the county land offices in California. In this way John and George Shipp registered all of Blayney Meadows, all of Double Meadows, several 40-acre parcels on the meadowy hillside from Sallie Keyes Creek all the way up Senger Creek to the first lake. Also the meadows near and around Sallie Keyes Lakes and, I think, on up to the lake below Selden Pass.

This surveying was done by the private registered surveyors of Fresno County and the County accepted the data and John and George Shipp shared several hundred acres by each having title to *every other* 40-acre piece. This "Whitney Survey" *gradually* put a stop to the disputes and many killings over mountain government range land in California.

At Blayney Meadows, it was 1925 before the official government surveyors arrived at Blayney. By that time, John and George Shipp had long discontinued their partnership in summer grazing of stock. They, however, still owned the property on a 50-50 basis and paid taxes accordingly.

The surveyors camped at lower Blayney all that summer and gradually accurately established land that was legally owned by the Shipps. All of the Sallie Keyes pasture and the hillside pasture from Double Meadow to upper Senger Creek was thrown out and declared NOT "swamp and overflow land."

A more accurate survey in our canyon was also needed because of the activity of the "robber barons" who were running wild in establishing claim to water rights in the San Joaquin drainage for the Los Angeles area power needs.

Maude Shipp apparently convinced John to re-file on all pasture land under the new survey. The new survey shifted all land one-quarter mile south and many of the quarter sections of the old survey were NOT "swamp and overflow" as they ended up on the side of Ward Mountain. George Shipp was not notified of these changes and ended up with only one 40-acre parcel which was still valid. John had quietly re-filed on all the rest of the valid parcels which were registered to him and had new descriptions. The only parcel still in George's name that was not cancelled was the one which we and the MacKenzie's now own.

Early spring in 1939 we finally located George Shipp living in Fresno. Dave MacKenzie and I made a date with him and went to see him at his home in the old college area of big homes and many shade trees just west of Van Ness, probably near the Fresno City College campus. We had a pleasant visit and told him our story about having a boy's camp at Blayney and that we were not sure what would happen when Jack Dusy bought the meadow.

ADDENDUM

An addendum to Fred's narrative about Blayney Meadows and how the Rosses and MacKenzies were lucky enough to own a bit of high Sierra Eden.

It's a shame that Fred ran out of gas before he was able to tell us more about early times in Blayney. I'll try to tie up a few loose ends, but my recollections may not be as keen as Fred's. I still have some gas left, as of this writing, but it has been mixed with cheap Scotch. So let the reader beware.

It was 1939 when Fred and I learned that John Shipp was about to sell his acres in Blayney to Jack Dusy. And it was Gertrude Berryhill who thought that John's bother, George, was owner of part of the original 240-acre homestead. (Gertrude was a delight-ful woman. A true autodidact, intelligent and well-versed in many areas. She lost her husband when we knew them. He suffered an appendix attack at the end of one summer in Blayney. He rode out on a horse to get medical aid but the appendix ruptured and he died a few days later. Gertrude moved to Nippinawasee in the Sierra foothills where Fred and I would visit to enjoy her wit and good company.)

Acting on Gertrude's hunch, we searched out deed records in Fresno. Sure enough, 40 acres of Blayney were in George's name. We called on George and told him his brother was about to sell his parcels to Jack Dusy. We asked if he'd be willing to sell his. "No reason not to", he said, adding that he'd never been back to Blayney since he had the falling out with his brother. "How much does he want for his land?" he asked. "Seventy five dollars an acre" we said. He said that sounded fair and agreed to sell. And he said he'd come up to Blayney the following spring to survey out the corners. This he did, doffing his good pants and wading around our "swamp and overflow" land in his long winter underwear. A sight one does not soon forget. A nice gentleman. Warm and friendly, unlike his brother.

Now our only worry, and not a small one, was how to come up with $3,000 to pay for our purchase. Not even a feeble minded banker would have loaned us a penny if he'd researched our financial resources. Fortunately, ever since coming from Scotland, my family had formed close ties with the Roths who lived at that time on the Stanford campus where Almon Roth, their father, was the university comptroller. So I approached Mr. Roth, hat in hand and quaking like one of our beloved aspen trees, to ask if he had a few bucks around not earning any interest. He listened to my pitch and miraculously agreed to buy, sight unseen, the property on condition that he would keep one-third while Fred and I could own the other two-thirds. We would then owe him $1,000 each with a 5% simple interest rate until the debt was paid off. We got the title to the land in 1940 after the survey was complete and George Shipp was paid in full.

It was probably a shocked Jack Dusy, our new neighbor, to find out that he was not the sole owner of Blayney Meadows. But he did not tell us. Most likely he was too embarrassed to admit that John Shipp had lied to him on who owned what when the purchase was made.

That Fred and I could never have been able to buy the property with our own money was evident in a letter Mr. Roth wrote to

Fred, carbon copy to me on March 15, 1950, a full ten years after the date of the sale. Mr. Roth wrote: "The property was purchased by me for yours and Dave's account on June 18, 1940 for $3,000. Interest on this amount since the date of purchase will amount to $1,467.90 as of April 1, 1050. According to my records, I have received total payments of $325 on the deal to date: $75 from Dave in 1943 and $250 from you in 1947." Mr. Roth goes on to politely ask us deadbeats whether we could find some other source to carry our debt. I think he felt the prospect of dunning us month after month was something he'd rather not face. We took his advice, found other resources, and paid off our obligation to him. When Al Roth died, he left his Blayney interest to his daughter and my sister-in-law, Miriam MacKenzie. So that's a fairly accurate account of how the Rosses and MacKenzies have the good fortune to have acreage in Blayney Meadows.

• David MacKenzie 2001

HIKE NUMBER 32
Florence Lake Trail

Category: Moderate
Length: 5 Miles Round Trip
Time: 3 Hours
Maps: U.S.G.S. Florence Lake and Ward Mountain Quadrangles

Directions From Shaver Lake

From the hardware store in the center of the village of Shaver Lake, travel northeasterly on Route 168 for a distance of 20.4 miles to the junction of the Kaiser Pass Road. Turn right at the Eastman Visitor Center and proceed to climb to the top of Kaiser Pass.

From the top of the pass in Badger Flat (24.6 miles), continue straight to meet Primary Forest Road 80. Continue intrepidly toward Florence Lake (18.7 miles). Expect slow progress on this narrow and windy road. Two hours from Shaver Lake is reasonable to expect. In times of heavy traffic, up to one additional hour may be required.

Parking

There is, generally, plenty of parking in the large lots just above the lake. Respect the parking as it is locally designated.

General Description

This is a fun outing! After driving in to the Sierra as far as it is physically possible, you are in the middle of one of the world's most spectacular geologic areas.

From late May/early June until the end of September, there is a ferry that operates from the "resort" to the opposite side of the lake. Beginning at 8:30 a.m. and running every two hours until 4:30 p.m., this ferry provides easy access to the far side of the lake and the beginning of this walk.

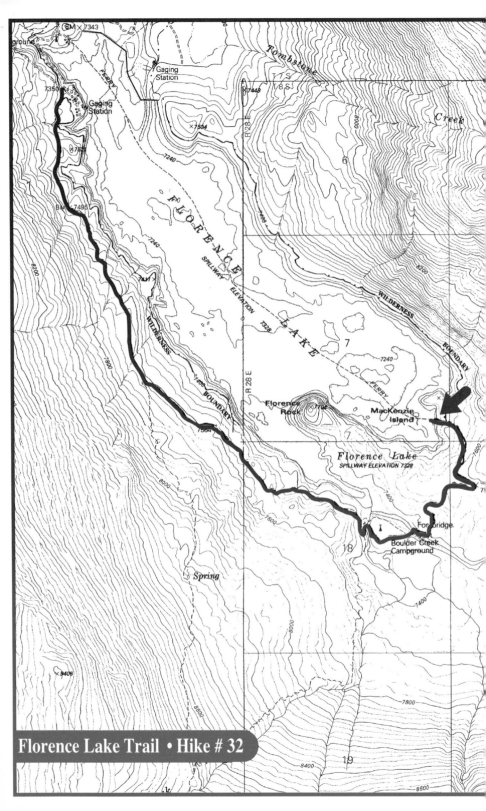

Florence Lake Trail • Hike # 32

The Route

Starting at the far side of the lake near the Lost Valley Pack Station "A" frame, the trail first follows the jeep trail in an easterly direction uphill across the shoulder of land marking the east flank of the lake. As you climb, you will approach a height of land at approximately 2,000 feet (.4 miles).

The high point of the beginning is reached at .5 miles. Turn south and lead down a small hill. Shortly you will reach the junction of the Florence Lake Trail. If you encounter a large green sign, you have missed the junction. Turn around and you will see it!

From the junction, walk .13 miles to the intersection of the jeep road and the Florence Lake Trail. The trail is marked with fairly fresh blazes on the lodge pole pines in the trail. Head northwest. At 1.2 miles, you will find a well-constructed wooden bridge. Cross the South Fork of the San Joaquin River here and follow along your route. We found the trail a bit confusing at this point. The horse trail clearly leads to a ford in Boulder Creek. As we found the intersection of the horse trail and the footpath a bit farther along (1.5 miles), we inspected the trail called 30E01.2! We found the reason the horses favor the ford. The bridge over the creek is unfit for horses. My advice is to just take the ford in dry weather, but in the spring freshet, find the way to the footbridge on 30E01.2!

From the intersection, continue northerly on the Florence Lake Trail. The sign at the intersection reads "4 miles" to the end. It is really only 3.56609 miles! But what a fine three and a half miles ahead. The trail climbs the western shoulder of Florence Lake and you will have wonderful views in all directions to accompany you back to the parking lot at the resort.

Spectacular among the views is the rocky overlook encountered at 4.2 miles. As you peer over the aspens below, the dam and the lake are just ahead. Continuing another .4 miles you will see two cabins below you to your right. This means you are just about to leave the woods and join the paved road (4.7 miles) that leads you left, back to the parking area (5.0 miles).

Cautions

Except for the trail disclaimer between the bridges near the start, the only caution concerns route finding at the beginning of the walk. The trails leading up from the lake have been well traveled and can be confusing. Keep the lake over your right shoulder and you should see some cairns to make your route finding easier.

Special Attractions

This is a lovely introduction to the Florence Lake region. From the lake you can also explore Blayney Meadows and the wilderness areas beyond. As you pass through Blayney, stop in at the Lost Valley Pack Station. The Ross family is one of the last families to offer burro rentals for backcountry exploration. You may find this animal to your liking as an adjunct to your mountain adventure!

HIKE NUMBER 33
Blaney Meadows

Category: Moderate
Length: 10.4 Miles Round Trip
Time: 6 Hours
Map: U.S.G.S. Florence Lake and Ward Mountain Quadrangles

Directions from Shaver Lake
From the hardware store in the middle of downtown Shaver Lake, drive north 20.4 miles to the Eastwood Visitor Center at the junction of the Kaiser Pass Road. Turn right toward Florence and Edison Lakes and drive up the pass 6.8 miles to the height of land. Continue slowly and intrepidly for approximately 15 miles to the parking lot at Florence Lake.

You can make this trip in approximately two hours from Shaver Lake. However, in times of construction, logging, or other delays, the time may extend an hour or more. Be patient with this road. It is not I-5!

Parking
Parking is ample at the trailhead. Bathrooms are also available.

General Description
This beautiful summer day, I was joined by the Elder Hostel crew walking into the Ross family's Lost Valley Pack Station. This group was excited to be able to spend a week in this beautiful section of the Sierra.

After riding across the lake on the ferry, we enjoyed a leisurely two-hour stroll into the meadow. Wildflowers were at their peak, and the views of Mt Shinn and Ward Mountain were awesome! I'd give this hike very high marks because of the view, altitude, and beauty of the mountain! This is a very rewarding hike to one of my favorite destinations!

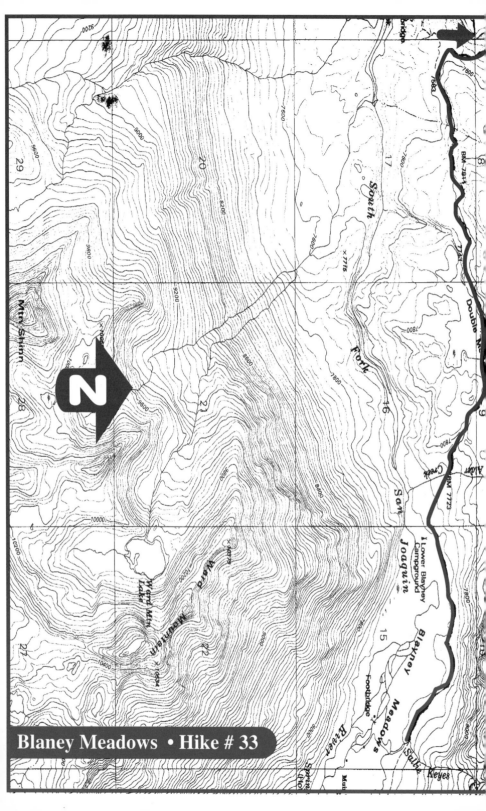

Blaney Meadows • Hike # 33

The Route

Starting at the ferry drop spot, walk up the jeep road past the Lost Valley Pack Station "A" frame. The trail roughly follows the jeep trail uphill in an easterly direction to the top of the ridge (.4 miles). At the height of land, head downhill slightly and meet the junction of the Florence Lake Trail (.5 miles). Turn left and follow the trail east toward Blaney. At .9 miles the trail will achieve its final plateau and reward you with nice views of Ward Mt. and Mt. Shinn.

At 1.2 miles, you will pass through a meadow of tule grass. This grass is often browsed by deer and passing burros. Continuing along, descend through a small spring decorated with Bigalow Sneeze Weed, Loepard Lillies, Columbine, and False Salomon Seal.

After walking through an interesting aspen grove, lower Double Meadow is reached. This meadow features Shooting Stars and Wild Onion. Shortly (1.9 miles) you will cross Tombstone Peak Creek. This is followed by Alder Creek's two separate branches. Those desiring a campsite will find one downstream from the main trail alongside the creek.

At approximately 3.0 miles, you will reach the first of the areas drift fences. These fences are important to keep closed because they contain free grazing horses and burros. Shortly past the drift fence, the trail branches off to the left toward Kings Canyon Park, Seldon Pass, and the public hot springs.

Continue along this trail through a lovely Juniper Grove. Cross Senger Creek and note the Chinquipin. The trail switches back and forth. On the second switchback, follow the creek upstream to a waterfall. Just above the falls is the intake for the Muir Ranch penstock. This supplies water for the hydropowered turbine which powers the ranch.

Continuing along the trail, the junction of the Muir Trail is soon reached. Here turn right and continue back toward the Muir Ranch. In a short distance, you will come to a sign indicating the trail down to the river.

In .25 miles, cross the river and head both inland and downstream. You will enter a large meadow containing the public hot spring.

Just behind the spring lies Warm Lake (5.2 miles). Enjoy.

Cautions
Trail finding is a bit of a challenge in the beginning of the walk because of the road and trail intersections. Watch for cairns, and if you are in doubt, retrace your steps.

Special Attractions
This is filled with nice surprises. Wildflowers, the hot spring, and if you are lucky you will meet one of the Ross family! The Ross family has been in Blaney Meadows since the 1930's, and the latchstring is always out!

THE SIERRA FOOTHILLS

As you drive from the valley floor to central Sierra, you will pass through the magical foothills. The foothills have a beauty of their own, and in the last few years, thanks to the work of the Sierra Foothill Conservancy, interest in the appreciation and preservation of this land has increased dramatically. In this last section, we present two foothill walks that have special interest and charm. For days that the long trek to Shaver does not delight, or on those wonderful spring days when foothills beckon, these walks are for you! The first hike, Black Mountain, is restricted to organized walks. Information concerning Black Mountain walks can be obtained from the Sierra Foothill Conservancy (559-855-3473). Squaw Leap is open to the public all year long.

THE SIERRA FOOTHILL CONSERVANCY

The Sierra Foothill Conservancy is a land trust whose mission is to preserve open space land in the foothills of Fresno, Madera, and Mariposa Counties. It is headquartered on Black Mountain, about midway between Prather and Tollhouse. Believing that foothill ranching is compatible with species protection, SFC accepts conservation easements from area ranchers who wish to protect their property from being subdivided where appropriate.

While SFC's the primary goal is to preserve living space for wildlife, it also helps to protect significant historic and prehistoric sites, provides a program of classes on natural history subjects for area residents, and encourages the use of its preserve lands by local schools and colleges.

In addition to these activities, SFC maintains a calendar of regularly scheduled hikes on its preserves during the cooler months. These hikes are free of charge and open to the public. You do not need to be a member of SFC in order to go on an SFC hike.

SFC's hikes range in difficulty from easy to strenuous as described in the following chapters. All are led by experienced volunteer docents. Many are scheduled to take place during peak wildflower displays. You can access these properties ONLY during regularly scheduled guided hikes since the preserve lands are working cattle ranches and are not normally open to the public.

To learn when the next hikes are to take place, or to obtain a schedule of activities, you can phone the SFC office at (559) 855-3473, visit the SFC home page at www.sierrafoothill.org.

HIKE NUMBER 34
Black Mountain

Category: Moderate
Length: 5.0 Miles Round Trip
Time: 2.5 hours
Map: U.S.G.S. Auberry

Directions from Auberry

This hike's directions begin from the bottom of the four lane: the junction of Route 168 and the Lodge Road. This T-shaped inter-section is marked by a large parking area and a slew of signs. Proceed on the Lodge Road toward Sierra High School for ap-proximately .4 miles. Turn right onto Black Mountain Road. Follow this good dirt road approximately 2.0 miles to a gate marking the entrance to the Sierra Foothill Conservancy's Black Mountain preserve. Members knowing the combination to the gate may drive the next 1.5 miles to the parking spot adjacent to the conservancy's caretaker's house. Those without member status may park at the gate and take benefit of the extra 1.5 miles of walking!

Parking

Parking is generally ample near the gated entrance to the preserve. Take care not to block the gate or its entrance.

General Description

The Mary Elizabeth Miller Preserve at Black Mountain is located on Black Mountain between Prather and Tollhouse, on the south side of Lodge Road. The mountain is clearly visible from portions of the Highway 168 "four lane" to Shaver Lake. The preserve covers 710 acres but may soon grow significantly with the addition of about 79 acres on the western flank of the mountain. You can reach the preserve by driving about three miles up Black Mountain Lane from the point where it joins Lodge Road, about four miles east of Prather. (Reprinted from the Sierra Foothill Conservancy's

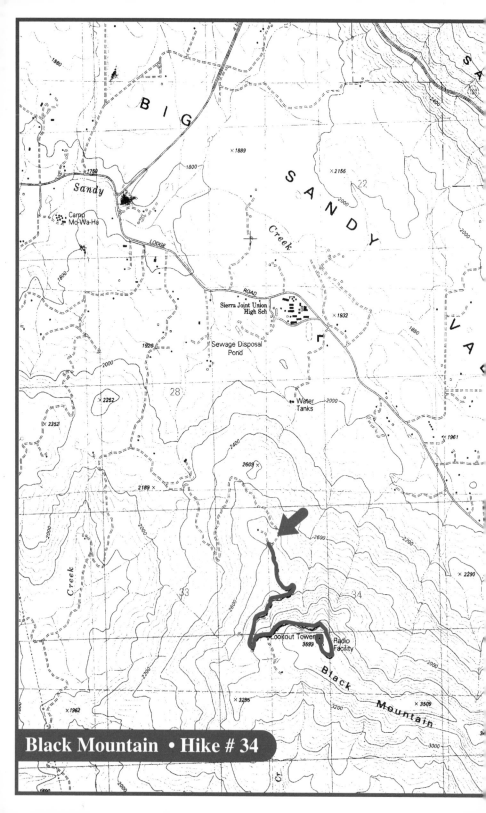

Black Mountain • Hike # 34

The Foothill Advocate: The Mary Elizabeth Miller Preserve at Black Mountain)
We found a perfect February day to be ideal for this mountain excursion. The road up from the caretaker's house is well shaded at this time of year, and the coolness of the day made for comfortable walking. We experienced blue skies above and overlooked the hazy fog typical of the valley in winter.
The hike itself carries you into a world of foothill history. The property was held by a family seeking utopian serenity during the early part of the twentieth century. Long abandoned, the site will still create euphoric and blissful rapture as you take in the beautiful sights along the way.

The Route
From the parking area near the caretaker's cabin, follow the road up hill. The road twists as it slowly ascends to meet the Loop Trail at 1.0 miles. We followed the road and easily reached the ridge trail in an additional .5 miles. Here we stopped and a few of the walkers took the short jog up to the summit to climb the fire tower. Abandoned after being replaced by satellite fire spotting systems, the tower stands as a tribute to the watchmen and women who spent many lonely hours looking for smoke.
From the ridge trail, we cruised the ridge top in a generally southeasterly direction. The ridge was easy to follow as it coursed up and down across the small hills comprising the ridge. In approximately one mile, we stopped for lunch and imagined the wildflower display that spring would provide!

Cautions
There are a few things to be on the lookout for in the foothills. First, poison oak is to be avoided, especially if you are allergic to the itchy beast. Although not an oak, this shrub can grow to a height of nearly ten feet. Consisting of three leaves in a cluster, the plant is best avoided. If you do get some on the plants oil on your skin, wash clothes and yourself as soon as possible.
In addition to poison oak, the foothills also are the home to ticks, scorpions, snakes, and a few other creatures that can range from

pesky to downright mean. Keep your eyes open and avoid confrontations with nature's friends.

Special Attractions
First, the honor to experience a walk on a property that has been purchased by and preserved by local friends of the land. Second, the sense of history that exists on this land. And, lastly, the absolutely beautiful views that abound in all directions! If you can, please support this vital foothill conservancy.

HIKE NUMBER 35
Squaw Leap Loop Trail

Category: Easy
Length: 2-6 Miles Round Trip
Time: 1 Hour
Map: U.S.G.S. Millerton Lake Quadrangle

Special thanks to Don Redmon for assistance with this trail description.

Directions from Prather
From the junction of Route 168 and the Auberry Road, drive east approximately one mile to the turn off for Auberry. Turn left and drive through Auberry. At approximately 2.8 miles, bear left toward North Fork. Continue for a total of 4.6 miles to the entrance to Squaw Leap, the Smalley Road, and travel 4.3 miles farther to the trailhead.

Parking
There is ample parking at the trailhead. At this location there is also a well-maintained toilet, picnic tables, and manicured lawns for play.

General Description
This is a segment of the Trans-Sierra San Joaquin River Trail reaching over 75 miles from Millerton Lake to the Pacific Crest Trail at Devil's Postpile monument. The trail runs through mostly open oak woodland and has good views of the river that it, at times, closely approaches. At about two miles you can cross a branch of Big Sandy Creek. The creek runs through a series of small caverns and caves. At three miles, the trail skirts a small parcel of private land and passes an old barn to the right. At this point, you can take a spur trail to the right for .5 miles to a beach area with a picnic table on the river.

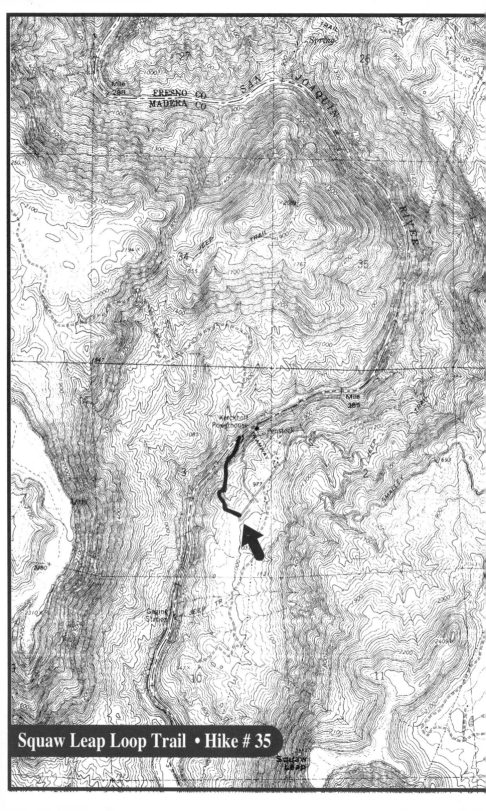

Squaw Leap Loop Trail • Hike # 35

The Route

Leaving the parking lot, head for the large Squaw Leap loop Trail sign just west of the lot. The trail meanders gradually through a grassy field as it descends toward the San Joaquin River. At 630 feet, you will pass a closed gate. These gates are for cattle control. Please close after you pass through.

At about .5 miles, the trail slabs north parallel to the river. Here glimpses of the river below appear to entice you.

At .8 mile, you will pass through a second gate as you make your final descent to the river. Just shy of the one mile mark, you will meet the bridge. This footbridge leads across the river to continue the loop trail or to reach Millerton Lake. The loop trail is approximately 9 miles in length. It does as it purports and leads you back to the river. The Millerton Trail is approximately 17 miles long and deposits the walker at Millerton Lake.

The short version (2.0 miles) from the parking lot to the bridge and returning makes a comfortable hour or two excursion. The longer treks require an early start and proper equipment, food, and water.

Cautions

Actually there are a few on this tame little walk. The Bureau of Land Management has done a good job of removing most of the poison oak from the trailside, however there were some plants in evidence on our walk. Know this plant and don't go near it!

The cave area is hazardous and is not recommend for entry except by experienced spelunkers. Being just under 1,000 feet in elevation, this hike is too warm for summer travel.

If you bring your dog, be sure to have a leash to keep them from grazing on the foxtails that line the route. My dog ate a few of the plants several years ago, and we had a miserable time of it!

Finally, this is tick, snake, and scorpion country. Don't be shocked to see one of these creatures on your excursion. They enjoy the flowers, too!

Special Attractions

Given the timing of nature and your schedule, this is one of the finest wild flower walks I've ever seen! The variety of flowers and their profuse distribution along the hillside truly intoxicate the walker. My guess for the best time of year would be from late March until early May, but each year is different. Your adventure will be to find the best time for you!

REFERENCES

Arno, Stephen F. (1973). **Discovering Sierra trees.** Yosemite National Park: Yosemite Association.

Greenberg, Ken; Thun, Jessie Myers; and Zylka, Claire Baird (1984). **Images of an age: Clovis.** Clovis, CA: Clovis Unified School District.

Hill, Mary (1975). **Geology of the Sierra Nevada.** Berkeley: University of California Press.

Manning, Harvey (1969). **Mountaineering: The freedom of the hills.** Binghamton, NY: Vail Ballou Press.

Rose, Gene (1987). **Reflections of Shaver Lake.** Fresno: World Dancer Press.

Spellenberg, Richard (1979). **The Audubon Society: Field Guide to North American Wildflowers.** New York: Alfred Knopf.

Storer, Tracy I. and Usinger, Robert L. (1963). **Sierra Nevada natural history.** Berkeley: University of California Press.

The Nature Company (1993). **Walking.** Seattle: Marquand Books.

Three-Forests Interpertive Society (1997). **Trail guide: Huntington Lake and Kaiser Ridge.** Prather, CA: Three-Forests Interpertive Assn.